Cross-Stitch Designs

from

India

First published 2004 by
Guild of Master Craftsman Publications Ltd
Castle Place, 166 High Street,
Lewes, East Sussex BN7 1XU

ISBN 1 86108 316 5

Publisher: Paul Richardson
Art Director: Ian Smith
Production Manager: Stuart Poole
Managing Editor: Gerrie Purcell
Commissioning Editor: April McCroskie
Editor: Dominique Page
Designed by Fineline Design
Set in Mahsuri Sans

Colour origination by Icon Reprographics
Printed and bound by Kyodo in Singapore

Please note:

Thread colour codes refer to the threads
used in the projects as shown in the
photographs. The charts and keys should be
regarded as reference only.

When a chart continues over more than one
page a generous overlap has been provided
to help you match the charts more easily.

CROSS-STITCH DESIGNS
FROM
India

Carol Phillipson

GUILD OF MASTER CRAFTSMAN PUBLICATIONS

Contents

Acknowledgements

Once again I am indebted to Ann for her ongoing help with the stitching and her unfailing enthusiasm, and to Alan for his unwavering support and help.

Many thanks also go to:

Coats Crafts UK
for their continuing help in providing all the threads and some of the fabric.
www.coatscrafts.co.uk
+44 (0)1325 394327

Willow Fabrics
for supplying the Zweigart fabrics.
www.willowfabrics.com
+44 (0)1565 872225

Framecraft Miniatures Ltd
for supplying pots, cards and accessories.
www.framecraft.com
+44 (0)1543 360842

Fireside Reflections
for the round footstool.
www.firesidereflections.net
+44 (0)1473 415705

GMC Publications would like to thank
Trading Boundaries
for kindly allowing the use of their premises and merchandise for the cover photography.
www.tradingboundaries.com
+44 (0)1825 790200

Introduction

Pablo Picasso was reported to have said, 'Art washes away from the soul the dust of everyday life'. How true that is of stitching, too. Life without stitching would certainly leave a huge void for me and for countless other stitchers too, I am sure.

I have spent the last eighteen months researching, designing and stitching from Indian art, architecture, textiles, ceramics, metalwork and crafts and it has been nothing other than pleasurable. What a wealth of diverse designs there was to inspire me. And it was perhaps fortunate that I had a deadline to keep to because I kept carrying on and on, right up to the last minute! I hope I have eventually provided you with a varied library of designs to use in your stitching.

There should be something for everyone, regardless of experience. Several of the projects are quite challenging and use other counted stitches too.

I hope that you gain a lot of pleasure from looking through the book, are inspired to use the designs and enjoy stitching and adapting them.

Materials, Equipment & Stitches

The basic tools that are required for you to stitch any (or all!) of the designs in this book are simple. I have used fabrics and threads that are all readily available, and have also included many small designs to use up odd pieces of fabric and any remaining threads.

General Accessories

Scissors are important. I have two pairs of needlework scissors: a small, sharp, pointed pair and a large pair. The small ones are only to be used for threads and I have even fastened a piece of wool on the handle to remind the rest of the family not to use them for anything else! I use the larger ones for cutting canvas, fabric and Vilene. I never use either of these for cutting paper, as this is notorious for blunting even the sharpest scissors.

Another useful item is a small pair of round magnets which fit on either side of the fabric that is being stitched and trap the chart, so that it stays in view at the edge of the embroidery frame. They also make a safe place to leave a needle. These are inexpensive and certainly invaluable.

A good light is an investment. There are many that are specifically designed for embroiderers and which often incorporate a magnifying glass, too. These are excellent, but do tend to be quite expensive. I have found that you need to have a good look round to find the light that suits you, as there are several different types. And do check that it will not get hot, as it can become uncomfortable when you are working under it for a length of time. If you haven't one of these special lights, a good, well-placed spotlight can be equally suitable.

Blunt-ended needles should always be used for counted-thread work, because they don't split the threads and weaken them. I find a size 22 or 24 ideal for evenweave and size 18 for canvas-work.

If you are stitching designs that include beads, and many of the projects in this book do, you will need a beading needle and most probably a simple needle threader in order to thread the beading needle! Most of the beads have too fine a hole to accept an ordinary needle.

Fabric

For each item in the book the fabric actually used is stated, but it can often be substituted by another. Where this may not work, I have given the exact name. I have used mainly Aida, Jobelan or Brittney and canvas. Aida is the easiest to use, but many stitchers, including myself, prefer to work over two threads on the finer Jobelan. If you are substituting a different fabric, remember that the higher the thread count, the finer the stitching becomes.

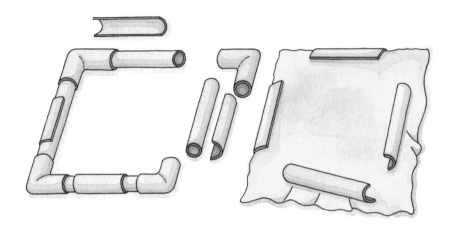

A clip-frame

Threads

The majority of the projects in the book are worked either in stranded cotton or tapestry wool, and many incorporate touches of metallic thread, but I have also included some variations, either for the colouring or texture. I find the wide range of threads and colours available a never-ending source of inspiration. I still have the 'zing' factor when I receive a bundle of new threads, even though I have ordered them!

The thread amounts given in the book are approximate, but where more than one quarter of a skein is needed I have put 'one skein'. Where less than this is required I have put 'small amount' as you may well have this amount left over from a previous project. I have used many of the same colours throughout the book.

Frames

The use and type of frames is a personal matter. Some stitchers never use one, while others always do. Although it is tempting sometimes not to bother, I am one of the people who always use one, because I find the end result more pleasing. It certainly minimizes the need for stretching and adjusting at the end.

Although I have a number of different frames, I really only use three. All my canvas-work and large projects are now done on clip-frames. These are a recent development and are a collection of lightweight plastic tubes and clips that can be made into a variety of sizes. The fabric is simply laid over the frame and tensioners are placed over to keep it in place. A simple twist adjusts the tension. They really have taken the hard work out of putting fabric on a frame and, moreover, they don't damage or mark the fabric. For smaller evenweave designs I used to use a hoop frame, either a wooden seat frame, which leaves both hands free for stitching, or a plastic flexi-hoop for very small items, but as clip-frames have become available in smaller sizes, I find that I tend to use these most of the time.

First leg of cross stitch

Completion of cross stitch

Stitches

Half-cross stitch

Although the designs use mainly full or half-cross stitch, I have included some other simple counted-thread stitches to give a variety of texture and interest. If you have not attempted to use these stitches before, do have the confidence to try them, as they are all easy stitches. However, before stitching the actual project, it would be wise to try them out on a scrap piece of material so that you can get the stitch and the tension right.

Rhodes Stitch

Bring the needle up from the wrong side at 1, go down at 2, come back up at 3, go back down at 4 and repeat this pattern until the stitch is complete. Always work the first stitch in the same direction, starting at the bottom left-hand corner. In the charts, the diagonal line indicates the first stitch.

Rhodes stitch

Eyelet Stitch

Bring the needle up from the wrong side at 1, go down into the centre, come up at 2, go down into the centre, come up at 3 and continue until the stitch is complete. As you work, pull the thread fairly firmly so that the centre hole is clear. Always start at the bottom left-hand corner.

Scottish Stitch

Bring the needle up from the wrong side at 1, go down at 2, come up at 3, go down at 4 and continue until the stitch is complete.

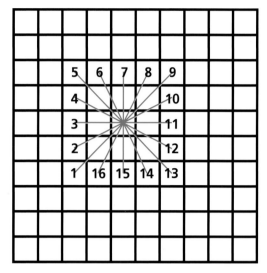

Eyelet stitch

Scottish stitch

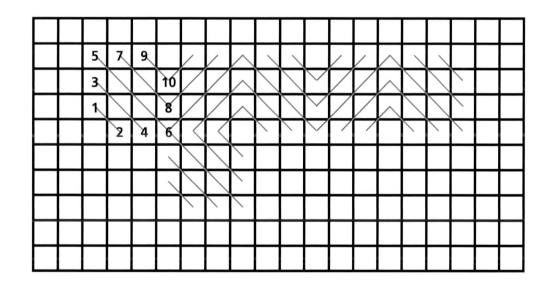

Adapting Designs

My aim during the writing of this book, as well as to give inspiration and interest to the stitcher, was to provide every reader with a 'library' of Indian patterns to be used wherever they are needed. The stitched pieces have been made up into various objects and the details of the charts, thread colours, thread counts and fabrics used have been given. I have tried to demonstrate different ideas to be used in your own stitched projects. It is important to plan before you start stitching if you are changing things and experimenting – nothing could be worse than the design disappearing off the side of the fabric because it isn't wide enough!

Charted designs can be worked on any fabric with even threads. These fabrics are known as evenweave and are said to have a 'count', usually expressed in tpi, which is the number of threads the fabric has per inch. For example, 14-count means that there are 14 threads to one inch (2.5cm) and, therefore, if you are working over every thread you will stitch 14 stitches for every inch. Similarly, if you work on 28-count fabric, but work over two threads, which happens quite often in the book, you are still working 14 stitches in one inch. Stitching a design on a fabric with fewer threads to one inch will enlarge the stitching, but you may then need an extra strand of cotton to cover the canvas or fabric. Always try stitching a small sample and adjust it before starting the main project. Conversely, if the thread count is greater, the work will be smaller, and may need less thread.

One obvious example of this are the peacock designs found on pages 40–43. The same chart, when worked on 12-count canvas in wool is suitable for the footstool, whereas a 19-count evenweave makes a smaller cushion centre.

To calculate the size of a stitched piece, take the pattern size (stitches) and then divide it by the number of threads per inch (2.5cm) of the fabric.

As an example, a design with 22 squares will be:

1in (2.5cm) when stitched on 22-count (22 divided by 22)
1¼in (3cm) – 18-count (18 divided by 22)
1½in (3.8cm) – 14-count (14 divided by 22)
2¼in (5.6cm) – 10-count (10 divided by 22)

Other ways to make the stitching fit a larger frame are to add a border or a card mount.

Colours are a personal choice. The colours in my designs are typically Indian, but they may not be your choice, or they just may not suit your colour scheme. Don't be afraid of changing them. It is usually more successful if you try to keep the darker tones in my designs as the darker tones in yours.

Altering the type of thread, by adding some metallic gold or soft cotton or perlé

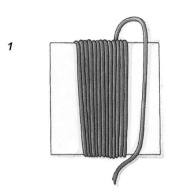

1

3

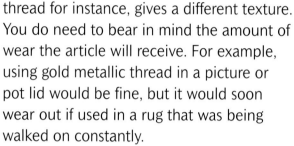

2

thread for instance, gives a different texture. You do need to bear in mind the amount of wear the article will receive. For example, using gold metallic thread in a picture or pot lid would be fine, but it would soon wear out if used in a rug that was being walked on constantly.

One of my favourite parts of designing is adding the finishing touches. Adding a few beads, a tassel, a twisted cord or a lace edging costs very little and doesn't take long, but it can make a considerable difference to appearance of the completed stitching. Many Indian articles are decorated with tassels, shisha mirrors, sequins or beads, so I had a wonderful time embellishing the stitched articles.

Making a Tassel

4

Take a piece of card slightly longer than your tassel is to be. Wrap thread around the card until it is fairly thick (1). Loop a piece of thread between the card and the wound threads at the top, pull it tight and knot it. Then cut the threads from the card at the bottom (2). Smooth the threads down and tightly wind a new length of thread to form a tassel (3). Using a needle, thread the end down so that the secured end becomes part of the tassel. Use the thread at the top to fasten the tassel to the stitching (4).

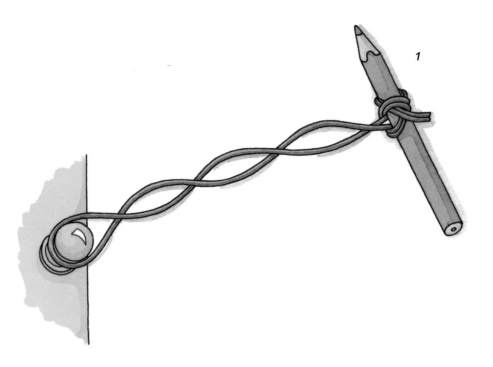

Making a Twisted Cord

First decide how long it needs to be. Always make it a bit longer than you really want it, because it is easy to trim. I cut the threads three times the required length of the cord, and half as thick as I would like the cord to be. Fasten a knot at both ends then thread one end over a door handle and thread a pencil through the other (1). Keeping it fairly taut, twist the pencil round and round the same way until it is tightly twisted. Take hold of the twisted thread in the centre and put the two ends together (2). The cord will automatically twist on itself. Remember to keep it taut as you bring the ends together, then it will twist evenly.

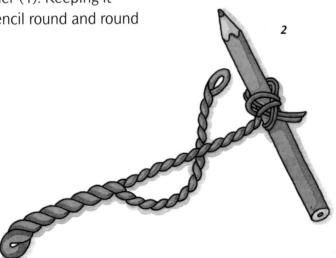

Helpful Hints

- Always be well prepared before you start.

- Don't use very long lengths of thread. Instead of saving time, these become frayed and ragged and need replacing. I find that approximately 16in (45cm) tapestry wool, 12in (30cm) crewel wool, 15in (40cm) stranded cotton and 12in (30cm) of metallic and silk thread give the best results.

- From time to time let the needle hang free at the back of the work to allow the thread to untwist.

- When the work is left on the frame, cover it with a cloth (a tea towel will suffice) to keep it free from dust.

- If the work is likely to be left for more than a few days, it is advisable to release it from its frame so that it doesn't become marked.

- While you are stitching, occasionally slide the needle along the thread slightly to even up the wear on the thread by the needle.

- Try not to take a break from stitching in the middle of long stretches as the tension of your stitching may vary slightly when you return to it.

- Don't carry thread across distances of more than three or four threads at the back, as this causes bulk and can distort the work.

- Always finish off each end of thread, so that there are no loose ends at the back to become tangled and caught in the stitching.

- When tapestry work is complete, hold it up to the light to see if any stitches have been missed and, if so, fill them in.

Designs from Metalwork and Leatherwork

During the Mughal period, many functional and decorative objects were made using metalwork, particularly brass, which were often intricately engraved and inlaid with wonderfully detailed patterns.

The craft involved a process known as lost wax metal sculpting, and this has now been developed to a fine art in India. It involves creating a wax version of the intended finished piece and then covering it in clay. This is then fired, which causes the wax to melt, leaving a hole in which molten metal is poured. When the metal has cooled, the mould is broken and the solid cast emerges. Details are then engraved and features chiselled to create the finished piece.

Many pieces are then also enamelled. This is done by pouring enamel dust into grooves made in the metal and then placing the piece in a hot furnace, which melts the dust, spreading it evenly through the grooves.

Leatherwork, an old Indian craft, was used for footwear, floor coverings, hookah bowls, animal trappings and also oil, ghee and rice containers. Skins and hides of camels, buffaloes, goats and horses were utilized in this way.

Today, camel hides are used to create artefacts such as vases, lamp bases and bowls, which are intricately painted with a dark background in an art form called 'naqqaashi'. After the hide has been cleaned and bleached it is stretched and pasted on a clay mould that has dried. When the hide is dry, the clay is broken and removed, leaving the hide in the shape of the mould.

The exquisite patterns and motifs that feature on Indian metalwork and leatherwork provided the inspiration for the designs in this section.

Vase Bell-Pull

I find the shapes and patterns of Indian receptacles most attractive, so I took the opportunity to use some in this bell-pull. The vase that provided the inspiration for the motif at the bottom of the design was made from leather, but the others were of metal, so I have used a variety of metallic and shiny threads to emulate them.

Working the design

Overcast the edges to prevent fraying and then stitch the design in the centre of the fabric. Follow the instructions on page 168 for making up into a bell-pull. This design would also be suitable for a framed picture.

Materials required

Fabric: 26-count linen 33 x 8⁵⁄₁₀in (84 x 22cm)

Threads:
Anchor Lamé: 1 skein gold 300, red 318
Anchor Astrella: 4 skeins gold 300
Anchor Marlitt: 3 skeins 826, 1 skein 1030

To work the design

Fabric count: 26-count linen worked over 2 threads to give 13-count

Number of strands: Use complete threads unless otherwise indicated

Stitch count: 56 x 334

Design size: 4³⁄₁₀ x 25⁷⁄₁₀in (10.9 x 65.3cm)

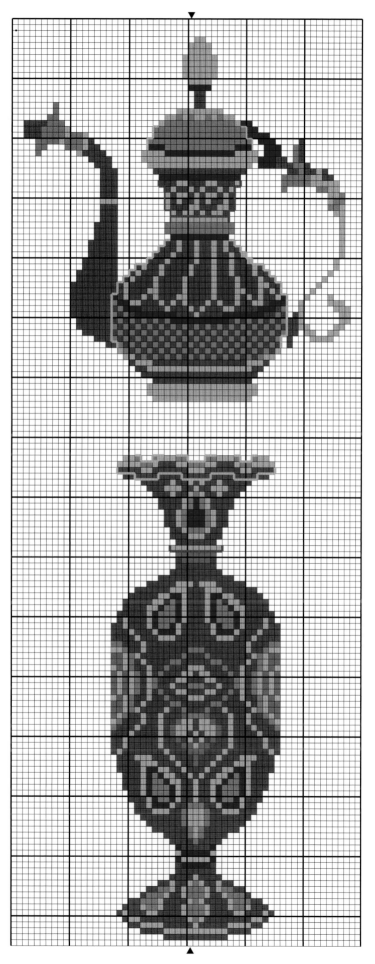

Designs from Metalwork and Leatherwork

Cross-Stitch Designs from India

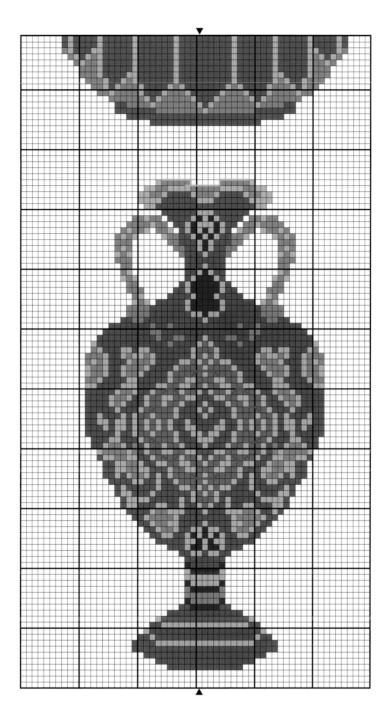

Thread required

▓	Marlitt 826
░	Astrella Gold 300††
▓	Lamé 318 Red††
▓	Lamé 300 Gold†/Marlitt 826
▓	Marlitt 1030
—	Marlitt 826*
⋯	Lamé 300 Gold*††
—	Lamé 318 Red*††

*Backstitch   †Use 2 strands   ††Use 3 strands

Blue and Gold Bookmark

These motifs, put together simply to form a very attractive bookmark, are typical of many that can be found throughout Indian art, textiles, metalwork and illuminated manuscripts. I adapted these particular motifs from enamelling and cloisonné work from Kashmir. The gold edging on the band matches the thread and tassel.

Working the design

Stitch the design in the centre of the Aida band, making sure that you have enough fabric left at the bottom for the sequin flower pearl to be attached. Turn in the top and bottom, then make a tassel approximately 2½in (6.5cm) long using lamé 300. Stitch this firmly onto the bottom of the bookmark and cover the fastening with a sequin flower pearl. Use a gold or frosted bead for the centre. I slip-stitched 2in (5cm) ribbon on the back to finish it off neatly.

Materials required

Fabric: 2in (5cm) wide Aida band x 10in (25cm) long

Threads:
Anchor Stranded Cotton: 1 skein 1349
Anchor Lamé: small amount 300

Beads:
Mill Hill: Frosted Glass 62034 x 12

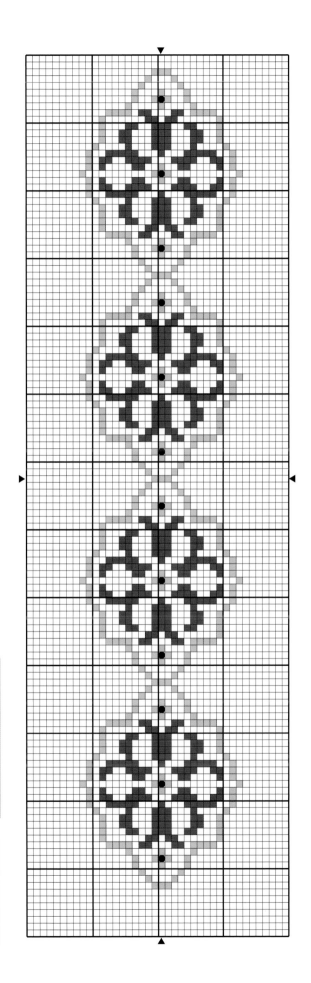

To work the design

Fabric count: 14-count worked over every thread

Number of strands: 2

Stitch count: 25 x 121

Design size: 1⁸⁄₁₀ x 8⁶⁄₁₀in (4.5 x 22cm)

Thread required

	Lamé 300 Gold††
	1349
	Mill Hill beads Frosted Glass 62034 x 12

††Use 3 strands

Turquoise Huqqa Designs

Two roundels at the top of an eighteenth-century enamel and silver huqqa from Lucknow were the inspiration for these designs. The use of gold, both on the edges and within the designs, is typical of Indian decoration. I chose to make the designs into a pot lid and a pot-pourri cushion. However, they would be suitable for many other projects; in particular, I think they would look very nice stitched onto cards.

Pot Lid

I used this design to decorate an elm pot that has an aperture of 3½in (9cm).

Working the design

First edge the fabric to prevent fraying, then work the design in the centre of the fabric. Once you have completed the stitching, iron Vilene on the back to strengthen the fabric and stop it from fraying when the circle is cut out.

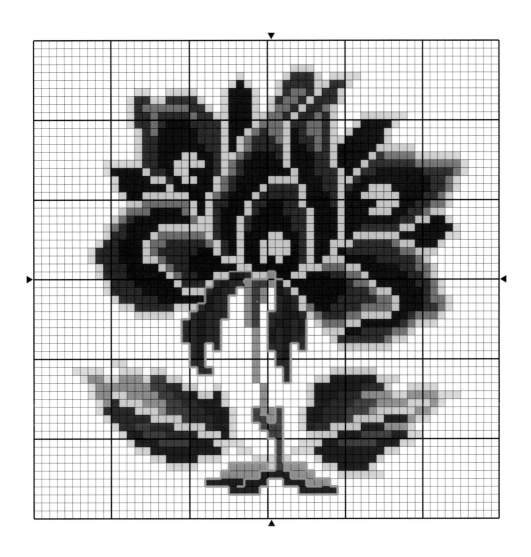

Materials required

Fabric: 19-count Easistitch

Threads:
Anchor Stranded Cotton: small amounts of
186, 188, 189, 175, 177, 178
Anchor Lamé: small amount gold 303

To work the design

Fabric count: 19-count worked over
every thread

Number of strands: 2 of cotton, 3 of Lamé

Stitch count: 57 x 54

Design size: $2\frac{7}{10}$ x $2\frac{8}{10}$in (6.8 x 7.2cm)

Thread required

■	189
■	188
■	188/186
■	186
■	178
■	177
■	175
■	Lamé 303 Gold††
—	Lamé 303 Gold*††

*Backstitch   ††Use 3 strands

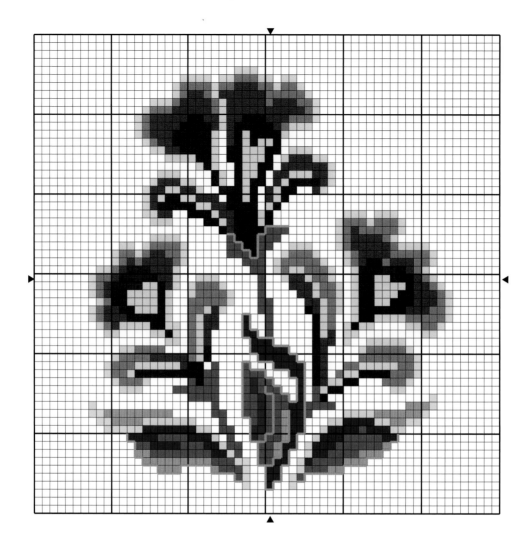

Pot-Pourri Cushion

I made this design into a 3½ x 4in
(9 x 10.5cm) pot-pourri cushion with a
green backing.

Working the design

Edge the fabric to prevent it fraying, then
stitch the design in the centre of the fabric.
Stitch gold braiding around the edge and
pull the ends through a chunky wooden
bead to form a tassel.

Tip

To straighten the 'curly' ends, hold them
over steam. But do take care: I use tongs to
stop my hands being scalded.

To work the design

Fabric count: 19-count worked over
every thread
Number of strands: 2
Stitch count: 47 x 53
Design size: 2⁵⁄₁₀ x 2⁸⁄₁₀in (6.3 x 7.1cm)

Materials required

Fabric: 19-count Easistitch 5 x 4⁵⁄₁₀in
(13 x 12cm)
Threads:
Anchor Stranded Cotton: small amounts of
186, 188, 189, 175, 177, 178
Anchor Lamé: small amount gold 303

Pot Lid and Pendant Design

These two designs were adapted from mid-seventeenth-century dagger sheaths of white jade with turquoise set in gold. They are delicate, yet detailed, designs, worked in a single strand of metallic Reflecta and lamé, which make a lovely lid for this tiny 32mm (1¼in) mahogany pot and centre for the pendant.

Working the design

Work the design in the centre of the fabric using a single strand over every thread then add the beads. Iron Vilene on the back of the design and make up as described in the manufacturer's instructions.

Materials required for pot lid
Fabric: 22-count 3 x 3in (8 x 8cm)
Threads:
Coats Reflecta: small amount 316
Anchor Lamé: small amount gold 303
Beads:
Mill Hill: Petite Glass 40557 x 4

To work the design
Fabric count: 22-count worked over every thread
Number of strands: 1
Stitch count: 25 x 27
Design size: 1⅒ x 1³⁄₁₀in (2.9 x 3.1cm)

Pot Lid

Thread required

■	Coats Reflecta 316
	Lamé 303 Gold
	Mill Hill beads Petite Glass 40557

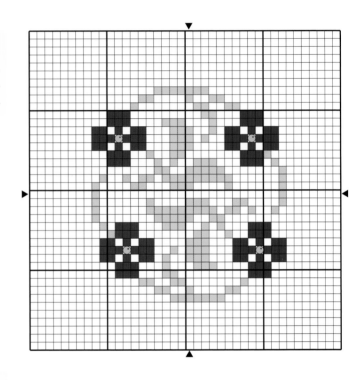

Pendant

Thread required

■	Coats Reflecta 316
	Lamé 303 Gold
	Mill Hill beads Petite Glass 40557

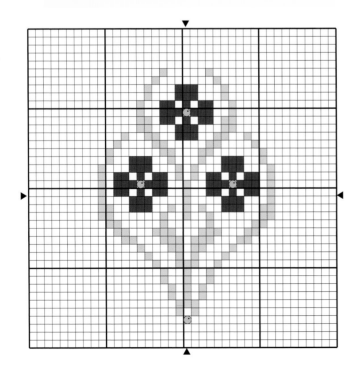

Materials required for pendant

Fabric: 22-count 3 x 3in (8 x 8cm)

Threads:
Coats Reflecta: small amount 316
Anchor Lamé: small amount gold 303

Beads:
Mill Hill: Petite Glass 40557 x 3

To work the design

Fabric count: 22-count worked over every thread

Number of strands: 1

Stitch count: 23 x 32

Design size: 1 x 1⁵⁄₁₀in (2.7 x 3.7cm)

Border Picture

I find the intricately engraved and inlaid metalwork border designs from early nineteenth-century India fascinating, because the patterns are so finely detailed. Originally, I had planned to use some of these to design several borders and motifs for individual items. However, I decided it would have more impact to combine several borders in one item to make either a bell-pull or a picture. If you wish, each border can still be used individually.

Working the design

Overcast the edges to prevent fraying, and then stitch the design in the centre of the fabric using two strands of cotton over two threads.

Materials required

Fabric: 28-count black Jobelan or Brittney 8 x 19in (20.5 x 48cm)

Threads:
Anchor Stranded Cotton: 3 skeins sunshine yellow 1304

To work the design

Fabric count: 28-count black Jobelan or Brittney worked over 2 threads to give 14-count

Number of strands: 2

Stitch count: 59 x 205

Design size: 4²⁄₁₀ x 14⁶⁄₁₀in (10.7 x 37.2cm)

See note on page 2

Cross-Stitch Designs from India

Thread required

████████ 1304

Designs from Textiles

The East India Company, founded in the early seventeenth century, was responsible for much of the trade of goods between India and the West. Painted and stencilled cloth from western India, embroidered silk and muslin from Bengal, cotton from south-eastern India and wonderful Kashmiri shawls were exchanged for precious metals and wine from Europe and the West.

The three main methods of decorating cloth are printing, weaving and embroidery, and I have used ideas from all of these in this chapter.

Textile printing is an ancient Indian craft, often used for clothes, curtains, bedspreads, wall- and tent-hangings. Block-printing, tie-dye and resist work are all methods employed to create designs. The most common fabric to be used for printing or inkwork is bleached cotton, as cotton plants grow so well in India's climate. The process for bleaching the cotton involves it being immersed in a solution of goat or buffalo dung, then rinsed well in a river. Natural dyes are still used in places, although chemical dyes are gradually taking over. Natural blue comes from indigo which grows in India, red comes from madder or alizarin, yellow is from myrobalan flowers, green is from an application of yellow overlaid with indigo, and a mixture of iron salts is used to create black.

Hand-weaving and spinning are some of the earliest crafts, and although a certain amount of mechanization has taken place, they still continue today. Traditionally, men did the weaving and women the spinning. Simple floor and bed coverings are still woven, mainly using simple pit-treadle looms, where the weaver sits on the ground, in the shade outside his home, and works the peddles of the loom from a dug-out pit.

One of the most-prized and well-known exports of Indian weaving is the Kashmir shawl, which is so fine and soft it can be pulled through a wedding ring. It was made from the wool of pashmina mountain goats from the Himalayas. In order to survive the extremely harsh winters, the goats grow an additional fleece under the outer hair and this forms the pashmina wool. Wild goats gave the best wool but, for practicality, most Kashmir shawls were from domestic pashmina goats. Sadly, once again, this craft has suffered from the introduction of mechanical looms, so only a few of these shawls are still woven. They are often beautifully embroidered and highly prized – and therefore very expensive.

Beautiful silk saris and scarves are also woven in India. They use both wild and cultivated silk; the former is indigenous and grows near to the rivers, while there are cultivated mulberry groves higher up on the land.

Exquisite Indian embroidery adds a riot of colour and texture to the base material. It is mainly stitched on cotton or silk. Designs are passed down through families, so individual distinctive styles of embroidery occur in different areas. Many articles are densely embroidered, such as clothes for special occasions, door-, wall- and tent-hangings, quilt coverings and trappings for animals. These may then be further decorated with shells, shisha mirrors, sequins and buttons. In the nineteenth century, beadwork and appliqué also became a feature on some of the embroidery, with many beads coming from Africa. Much of the stitching is chain stitch, but long-and-short satin and herringbone are also found, and fine buttonhole stitch is used to attach shisha mirrors. Shisha mirrors are supposed to dazzle the 'evil eye' and blind it, keeping the wearer safe from harm.

Embroidered gifts are part of tradition. In some areas a bride's whole family will work to embroider her wedding dress in addition to fine articles for her new home. One tradition that used to be followed was that as soon as a baby was born, the grandmother started to embroider a very special tight-fitting shawl (phulkari) called a 'bagh'. The base fabric would be completely covered in beautiful embroidery. It took years to complete, and was then carefully wrapped and put away for the child's own wedding.

To enable patterns to be repeated accurately the craft of 'okair saazi', a form of stencilling, is used. It involves intricate, multiple-cutting of paper patterns, and they alone are very decorative. This is such intense work that the craftsmen have to stop working when they reach forty-five because their eyesight is not felt to be sharp enough for the required accuracy!

These printed, woven and embroidered textiles provided a marvellous source of design and colour for the following projects.

Peacock Footstool and Cushion

This bright, symmetrical design was adapted from the silhouette of a block-printed motif from Gujarat, near to the Arabian Sea. Many designs include the peacock because, in addition to it being so colourful, it represents Sarasvati, the Hindu goddess of poetry, music and wisdom.

It was such an attractive design that I also adapted it for use with stranded cottons and made a cushion centre. Colour references for stranded cotton are given in brackets.

Working the footstool

I mounted this design into a 12in (30cm) dark wood stool from Fireside Reflections, but if you are using a different stool, you will need to allow sufficient canvas to cover it. I have not stated the amount of wool required for the background as this will vary, and you may like to choose an alternative colour.

Stitch the design in the centre of your canvas using tent stitch over every thread

Footstool

❖ **To work the design**

❖ **Fabric count:** 14-count tapestry canvas

❖ **Number of strands:** 1 of wool

❖ **Stitch count:** 131 x 129

❖ **Design size:** 9³⁄₁₀ x 9³⁄₁₀in (23.8 x 23.4cm)

Cushion

❖ **To work the design**

❖ **Fabric count:** 19-count fabric worked over every thread

❖ **Number of strands:** 2

❖ **Stitch count:** 131 x 129

❖ **Design size:** 6⁹⁄₁₀ x 6⁸⁄₁₀in (17.5 x 17.2cm)

Thread required for both designs

	8166 (324)
	8000 (1)
	8694 (134)
	8692 (133)
	8690 (132)
	9392 (375)
	9324 (388)
	9274 (254)
	8964 (185)
	8744 (152)
	8972 (189)
	8968 (187)
	8612 (123)
	8808 (1089)
	8162 (326)

with wool. I recommend using a frame. Stretch the work back into shape, if necessary, then make up as appropriate to your stool. Most stools have a loose, padded centre that needs to be removed (usually by taking out a screw). Your work should be stretched over this and stapled to the base with the excess canvas cut off. The centre then needs to be fitted and secured back into the base.

Working the cushion

Overcast the edges to prevent fraying, then stitch the design in the centre of the fabric using two strands over every thread. Make it up either into a small cushion, larger cushion with a border, or a picture.

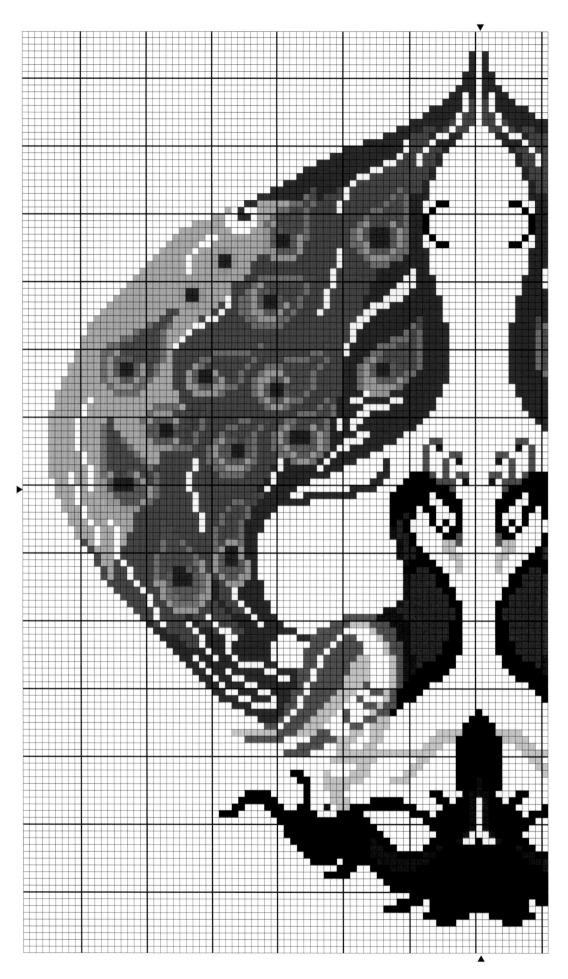

Cross-Stitch Designs from India

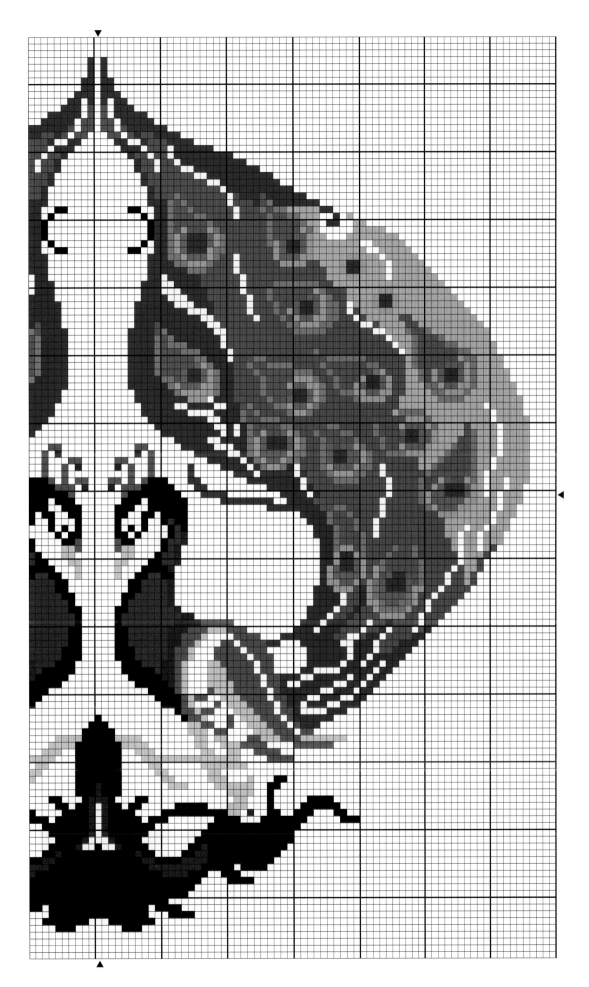

Tree-of-Life Picture

This design makes a striking picture. It was adapted and simplified from a large cotton tent-hanging. The tent-hanging was a typical Mughal prayer carpet design with a border, a mihrab arch at the top and beautifully detailed flowers. The ground at the base of the original was uneven and there was a smaller plant at either side.

Working the design

Edge the fabric to prevent it fraying and then stitch the design in the centre of the fabric.

Thread required

▇	1036
▇	1034
▇	1033
▇	376
▇	13/22
▇	11
▇	10
▇	276
——	1034*
——	13/22*

*Backstitch

Materials required

Fabric: 28-count Jobelan or Brittney 19 x 16in (48.5 x 41cm) allowing for the white border

Threads:
Anchor Stranded Cotton:
2 skeins 13, 22
1 skein 1033, 1034, 1036, 376, 11, 10, 276

To work the design

Fabric count: 28-count Jobelan or Brittney worked over 2 threads to give 14-count

Number of strands: 2

Stitch count: 107 x 157

Design size: 7⁶⁄₁₀ x 11³⁄₁₀in (19.4 x 28.5cm)

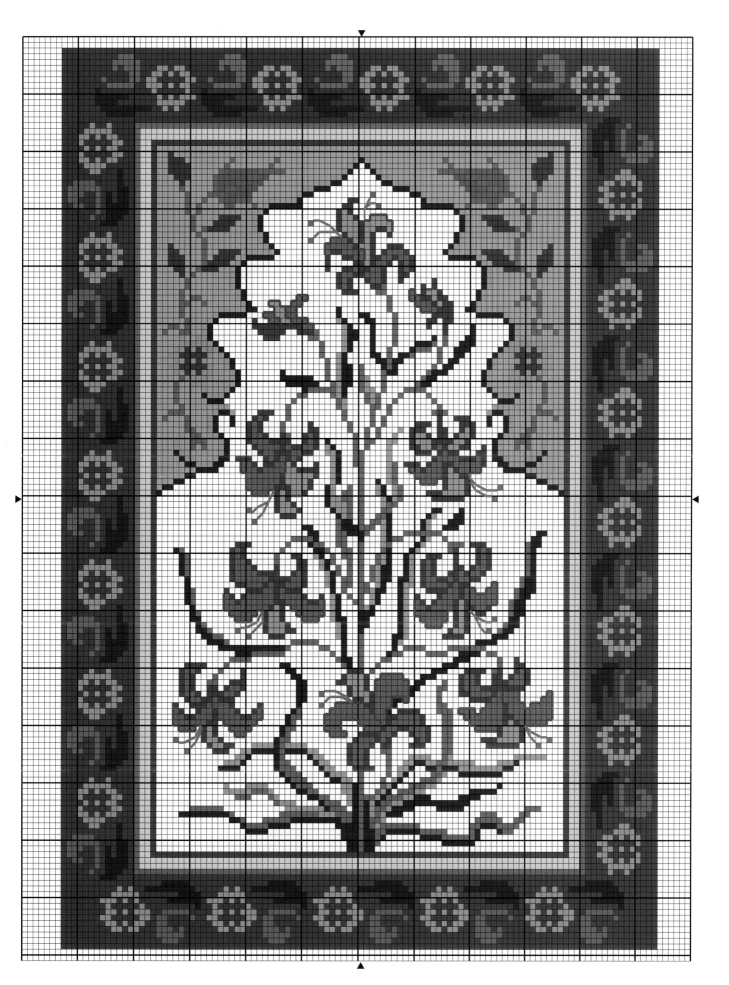

Tote Bag Border

This design was originally a decorative border on a cotton full-skirt, called a gaghra. The colours were almost identical to the ones I have chosen to use here. With a black background I felt it would make a very attractive bag. Indians do stitch bags for a number of uses, including tobacco bags and 'betel' bags. In certain areas of India these are ritually made by a bride to be given to the groom as part of an exchange of presents at their wedding. They are for storing betel leaves, which Indians chew with lime and nuts. Bags often have cowrie shells and tassels fastened to them, but I have changed these to beads on this bag.

The design could easily be adapted to any size by extending each repetitive border horizontally or stitching more black vertically. I added 28 rows at the bottom and 35 at the top for this bag. I then used a strong black cotton for the back of the bag.

Materials required

Fabric: 14-count canvas for the size of your project

Threads:
Anchor Tapisserie wool:
1 skein 8624
2 skeins 9506
3 skeins 9678, 8236
4 skeins 8002
5 skeins 9562
9 skeins 9800

Working the design

I recommend using a rectangular frame to keep the shape. Decide on your bag width then work the design in the centre of the canvas, repeating the design to the required width. For the backing, I used a heavy black twill cotton measuring 13 x 28in (33 x 71cm). Fasten the stitching across the twill, placing the top of the stitching 6in (15cm) from one end. Making a small hem, turn the 6in (15cm) forwards to cover the top of the

stitching and machine. Fold the twill ⅜in (1cm) from the bottom of the canvas and, with right sides facing, stitch up the sides. Turn it the right way round, then, making a small hem, turn in the top back. This gives you the basic bag. I added a black lining, beads at the base and the centre-top, and stitched a fastening with velcro. I plaited thin leather strips for a handle, but black twill handles would be equally appropriate.

Thread required

■	9800
■	9678
	8002
■	8236
■	9562
■	8624
	9506

To work the design

Fabric count: 14-count tapestry canvas

Number of strands: 1 strand of wool

Stitch count: 189 x 90

Design size: 13⁵⁄₁₀ x 6⁴⁄₁₀in (34.3 x 16.3cm)

▼

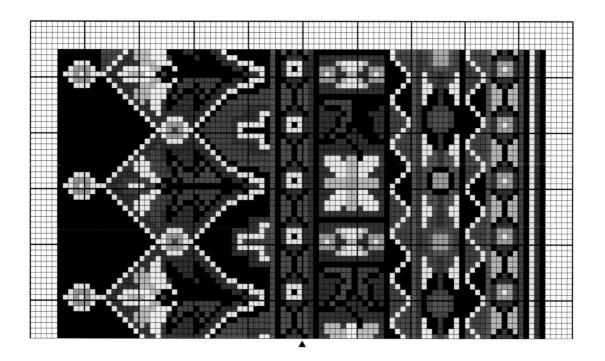

▲

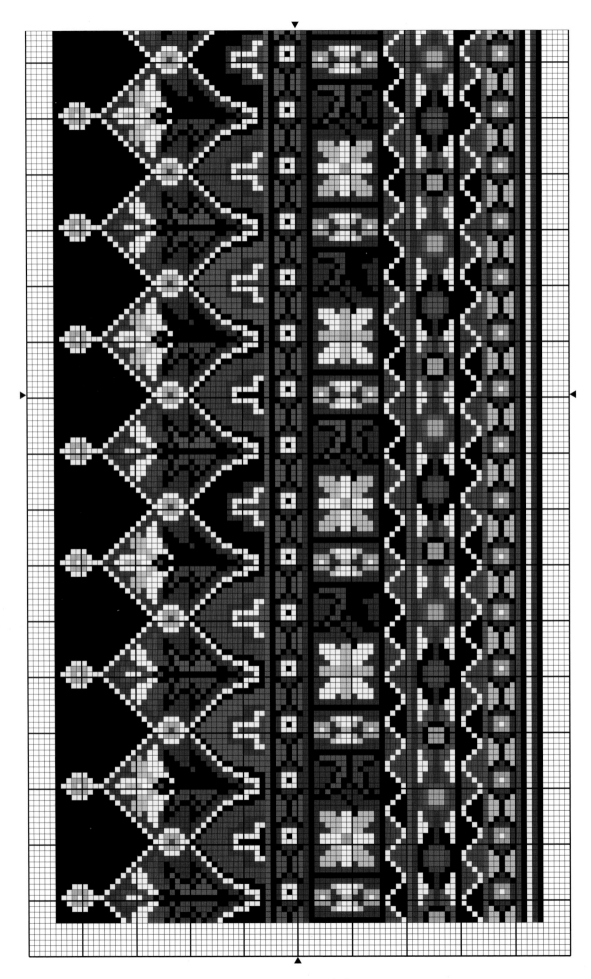

Cross-Stitch Designs from India

Ecru Flower Card

This pretty card design, taken from part of a tent-hanging, would make a very nice birthday or thank-you card. I was drawn to the colours used, and as the hanging was on an ecru background, I have followed suit, although it would also look nice on ivory or cream. I think stitching cards is a good way of putting small remnants of fabric to good use.

Working the design

Stitch the design in the centre of the fabric and then fit it into the card of your choice. I used a Metallic Linen Pearl card with an oval aperture of 5¼ x 3½in (13.3 x 8.9cm) from Impress Cards.

Materials required

Fabric: 28-count ecru Jobelan or Brittney 6 x 4¼in (15 x 11cm)

Threads:
Anchor Stranded Cotton: small amounts of 13, 11, 338, 878, 876, 127, 01
Anchor Lamé: small amount gold 303

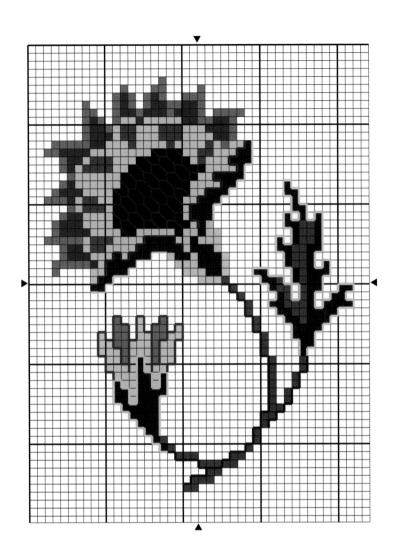

Thread required

▰	13
▰	11
▰	338
▰	878
▰	876
▰	127
▰	Lamé 303 Gold††
▰	Lamé 303 Gold*††
▬	13*†
▬	878*†
▬	01*

*Backstitch   †Use 2 strands   ††Use 3 strands

To work the design

Fabric count: 28-count worked over 2 threads to give 14-count

Number of strands: 2 of cotton, 3 of Lamé

Stitch count: 40 x 52

Design size: 2⁹⁄₁₀ x 3⁷⁄₁₀in (7.3 x 9.4cm)

Blackwork Picture

The inspiration for this design came from a tent-hanging that featured colours and patterns that reminded me of blackwork. It would look equally good made up as a picture or a bell-pull.

Working the design

If blackwork is new to you, don't be afraid to give it a try, as it is only cross stitch and backstitch. You could always try stitching a coaster first (see pages 53–55). The easiest way is to edge the fabric so that it doesn't fray, then work the design in the centre of the fabric, stitching first the outlines in two threads then filling in the patterns using one thread. Use two strands of lamé for backstitch and three for cross stitch.

Materials required

Fabric: 28-count Jobelan or Brittney
12 x 18in (30 x 46cm)

Threads:
Anchor Stranded Cotton:
1 skein 1029, 127, 102,
small amount 98, 87
Anchor Lamé: small amount gold 300

To work the design

Fabric count: 28-count Jobelan or Brittney worked over 2 threads to give 14-count

Number of strands: 2 of cotton, 3 of Lamé

Stitch count: 67 x 131

Design size: 4⁸⁄₁₀ x 9⁴⁄₁₀in (12.2 x 23.8cm)

Thread required

▨	98
▨	Lamé 300 Gold††
▨	1029
▨	127
▨	102
▨	87
───	1029*
───	102*
───	127*
───	Lamé 300 Gold*††

*Back stitch   ††Use 3 strands

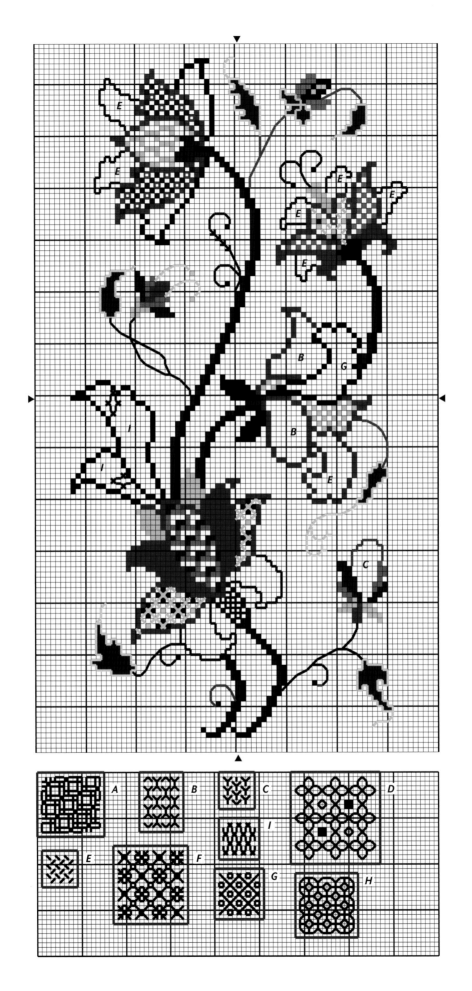

Cross-Stitch Designs from India

Blackwork Coasters

These designs are taken from the same source as the picture on page 51, but are quite quick to do and would make wonderful presents. They are worked on 22-count fabric and you can stitch all four from one skein of each colour. The colouring could easily be changed to match a tablecloth as long as the depth of colour is matched. I used a variegated thread for the patterns and it is most effective.

Working the designs

Work the designs in the same way as described for the bell-pull/picture on page 51. I found it practical to work all four on one large piece of fabric, as it is easier to

To work the design

Coaster 1
Stitch count: 59 x 39
Design size: 2⁷⁄₁₀ x 1⁸⁄₁₀in (6.8 x 4.5cm)

Coaster 2
Stitch count: 51 x 39
Design size: 2³⁄₁₀ x 1⁸⁄₁₀in (5.9 x 4.5cm)

Coaster 3
Stitch count: 54 x 37
Design size: 2⁵⁄₁₀ x 1⁷⁄₁₀in (6.2 x 4.3cm)

Coaster 4
Stitch count: 58 x 42
Design size: 2⁶⁄₁₀ x 1⁹⁄₁₀in (6.7 x 4.8cm)

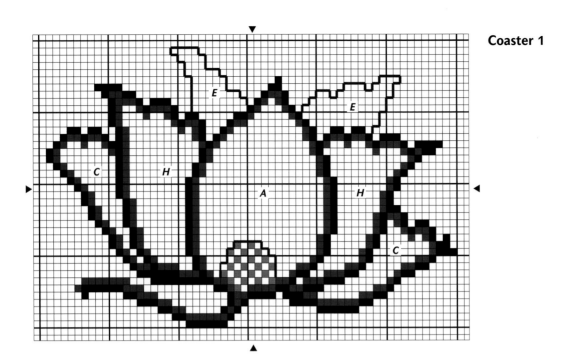

Coaster 1

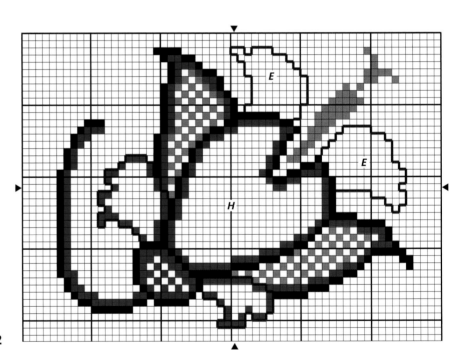

Coaster 2

handle a larger piece. Back them with
Vilene before cutting out the individual
designs. If you work them on one piece
of fabric, make sure that you leave enough
space between the designs to cut out each
individual coaster. I used coasters
measuring 81mm square (3¼in square).
They each had a clip-in back and took only
minutes to complete.

Coaster 3

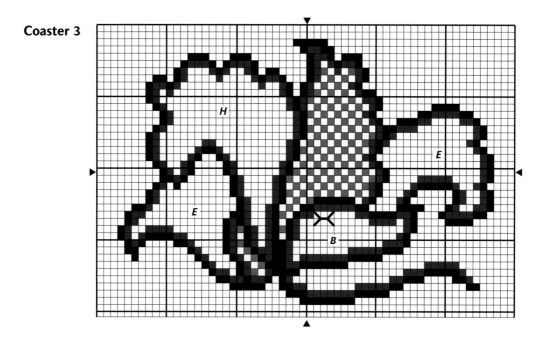

Coaster 4

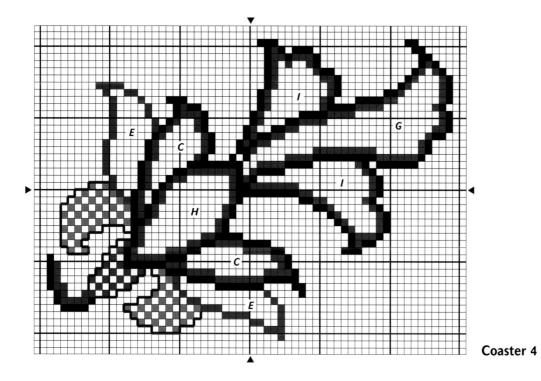

Thread required

▨	188
■	127
▨	Variegated thread
—	149*

*Backstitch

Orange Pot-Pourri Cushion

This colourful design was adapted from a fragment of a silk-embroidered shawl from Eastern Punjab. It is worked in half-cross stitch on 14-count canvas using stranded cotton, Marlitt and lamé, and includes Rhodes stitch. Beads or a tassel finish it off well.

Materials required

Fabric: 14-count canvas 8 x 8in (18 x 18cm)

Threads:
Anchor Stranded Cotton:
2 skeins 386, 46
1 skein 403, 334, 326, 45
Anchor Lamé: 1 skein 303
Anchor Marlitt: 1 skein 850, 2 skeins 864

To work the design

Fabric count: 14-count canvas

Number of strands: 12 of Lamé, 6 of Stranded and Marlitt. Note: Marlitt only has 4 strands, so you need to use 1 whole thread and 2 strands from another

Stitch count: 72 x 72

Design size: 5⅒ x 5⅒in (13.1 x 13.1cm)

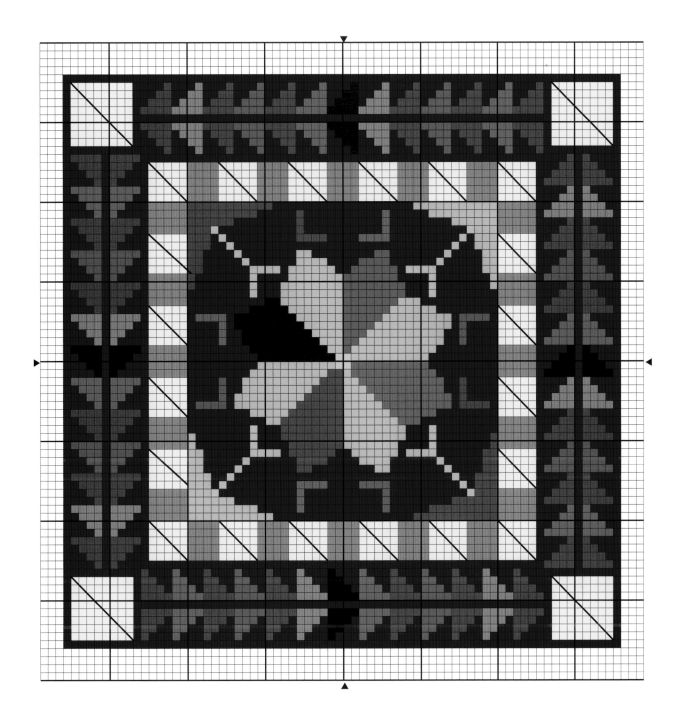

Working the design

Work the design in the centre of the canvas. You may find it easier to work the half-cross first, as the holes then become clear for the Rhodes stitches.

Thread required

	403†
	Lamé 303 Gold††
	334†
	Marlitt 850†
	326†
	46†
	45†
	Marlitt 864†
	386†
——	386* 1st stitch of each Rhodes stitch

*Backstitch   †Use 6 strands   ††Use 12 strands

Peacock Picture

This design is taken from a wonderful Mughal tent-hanging that features a mass of birds, plants, exotic flowers and insects, all in shades of red and green. I have pieced together fragments that particularly appealed to me to create this picture.

Working the design

Edge the fabric to prevent fraying, then work the design in the centre over two threads using two strands of cotton.

Materials required

Fabric: 28-count Jobelan or Brittney 15 x 25in (38 x 63.5cm) allowing for a white edge as in the worked picture

Threads:
Anchor Stranded Cotton: 1 skein of 45, 46, 47, 13, 269, 268, 266, 386
Anchor Lamé: 1 skein gold 303

Thread required

	386
	45
	47
	46
	13
	269
	268
	266
	Lamé 303 Gold††
	386/13
	45*
	269*†
	47*
	386*
	269 x 1*

*Backstitch †Use 2 strands ††Use 3 strands

Cross-Stitch Designs from India

Oval Pot Lid

The delicate design for this stitched lid was created by combining a pattern from a skirt border with a shape from a sixteenth-century illuminated page of the Koran. The aperture of the oval pot is 2¾ x 2in (7.5 x 5cm).

Working the design

Carefully stitch the design in the centre of the fabric. As it is so fine, I ironed Vilene on the back before stitching on the beads. Make up the lid according to the manufacturer's instructions.

Materials required

Fabric: 22-count evenweave 5 x 3⁵⁄₁₀in (13 x 9cm)

Threads:
Anchor Stranded Cotton: small amount of 230, 46, 334
Anchor Lamé: small amount 303, red 318

Beads:
Mill Hill: Petite Glass 40557 (gold) x 44

To work the design

Fabric count: 22-count evenweave fabric

Number of strands: 2 of Lamé, 1 of Stranded Cotton

Stitch count: 41 x 67

Design size: 1⁹⁄₁₀ x 3in (4.7 x 7.7cm)

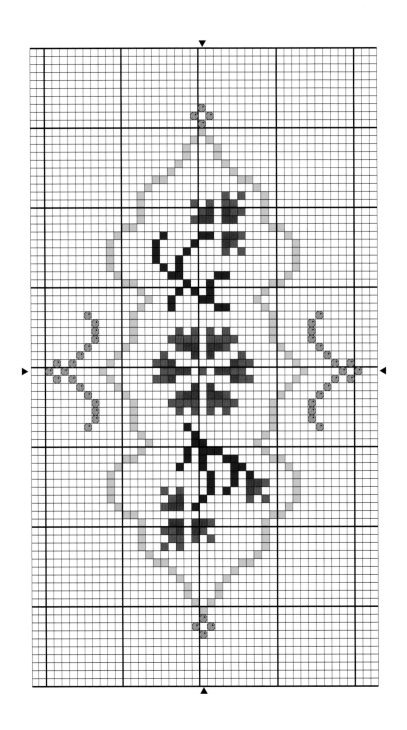

Thread required

▨	Lamé 303 Gold†
■	230
▨	46
▨	334
▨	Mill Hill beads: Petite Glass 40557

†Use 2 strands

Needlework Accessories

These designs were taken from a seventeenth-century tent-hanging. The pattern was so intricate that it was hard to pick out any individual items from a distance. However, when I looked closely I discovered that there were hundreds of small designs, some of them quite beautiful, so I have selected a few and put them together to make this set. I stitched the needlecase on ecru Jobelan then matched the thread for the background of the pincushion and scissor-keeper. The small designs would look attractive in cards too, and the border on the pincushion would be suitable for a photograph frame.

One skein of 47, 46, 316, 861, 859, 177 and three skeins of 852 of Anchor stranded cotton will stitch all three designs.

Needlecase
Working the design

Edge the fabric to stop fraying. Work the design in the centre of the right half of the fabric. Remember your needlecase opens like a book.

Pincushion
Working the design

Work this design in the centre of your canvas using tent stitch over every thread and three strands of cotton. Make up into a pincushion. I always add a tassel to pincushions so that they can be picked up easily, even when they are full of pins and needles. Make up following the directions on page 169.

Needlecase

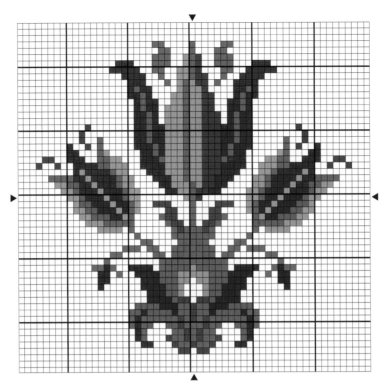

Pincushion

Needlecase

Materials required
Fabric: 28-count Jobelan 11 x 6in (28 x 15cm)
Threads:
See text

To work the design
Fabric count: worked over 2 threads to give 14-count
Number of strands: 2
Stitch count: 51 x 49
Design size: 3⁹⁄₁₀ x 3⁵⁄₁₀in (9.3 x 8.9cm)

Pincushion

Materials required
Fabric: 28-count canvas 6 x 6in (15 x 15cm)
Threads:
See text

To work the design
Fabric count: 22-count canvas
Number of strands: 3
Stitch count: 85 x 85
Design size: 3⁹⁄₁₀ x 3⁹⁄₁₀in (9.8 x 9.8cm)

Scissor-Keeper
Working the design

This useful item, made up into a tiny cushion and fastened to the handle of your scissors, either with a twisted cord or a bought cord, will make your scissors easier to find. Stitch the design in the centre of the canvas in tent stitch using three strands and working over every thread, using 852 for the background and two additional rows all the way round. Make up into a cushion as described on page 169. To finish, I added a border by working a satin-stitch edge over four strands, then stitched on a cotton backing and padded it. As the cushion is so small, I made the end of the twisted cord into a tassel, so that it can easily be picked up.

Scissor-Keeper

Materials required
Fabric: 28-count canvas 2 x 2in (5 x 5cm)
Threads:
See text

To work the design
Fabric count: 22-count canvas
Number of strands: 3
Stitch count: 19 x 19
Design size: 1³⁄₁₀ x 1³⁄₁₀in (3.4 x 3.4cm)

Thread required

	47
	46
	316
	861
	859
	177
	852

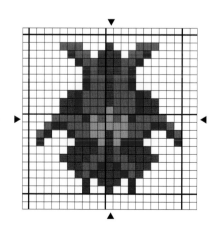

Gift Bag Motif

This attractive motif will make a small gift even more special.

Working the design

Stitch it onto the front of a ready-made 14-count gift bag (or make one yourself from Aida) and tie the handles with ribbon. It would also look nice stitched in cream with cream ribbons, or silver with white ribbons for a wedding gift or a bridesmaid's token.

Materials required

Fabric: 14-count ready-made bag from Framecraft

Threads:
Anchor Stranded Cotton: small amounts of 87, 98, 100, 102
Anchor Lamé: small amount gold 303

Beads:
Mill Hill: Glass Seed 02011 x 10

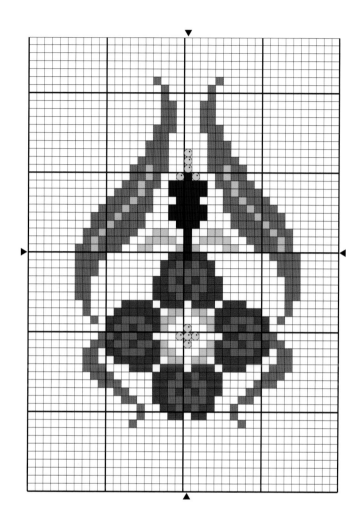

To work the design

Fabric count: 14-count

Number of strands: 2 unless otherwise indicated

Stitch count: 29 x 44

Design size: 2¹/₁₀ x 3¹/₁₀in (5.3 x 8cm)

Thread required

	102
	98
	100
	87
	Lamé 303 Gold†
	Mill Hill beads Glass Seed 02011

†Use 3 strands

Green and Gold Bookmark

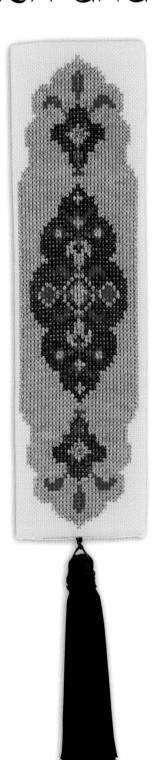

Adapted from a large textile design, this makes a lovely bookmark but it would also be suitable for a door fingerplate. Within the original design there were similar motifs containing maroon and dark purple colours. If you wish, these colours could replace the blue in this design. The green background is worked in a single thread to enable the shapes to be more prominent.

Working the design

Overcast the edges to prevent fraying, then stitch the design in the centre of the fabric using the threads as indicated. I ironed Vilene on the back and then stitched a dark blue tassel at the end. You could make a tassel using some of the 123 thread used in the design.

Materials required

Fabric: 28-count Jobelan or Brittney or 14-count Aida 10 x 4in (25.5 x 10cm)

Threads:
Anchor Stranded Cotton: 1 skein of 843, 123, small amounts of 46, 280
Anchor Lamé: 1 skein gold 300

Beads:
Mill Hill: Glass Seed 02011 x 4

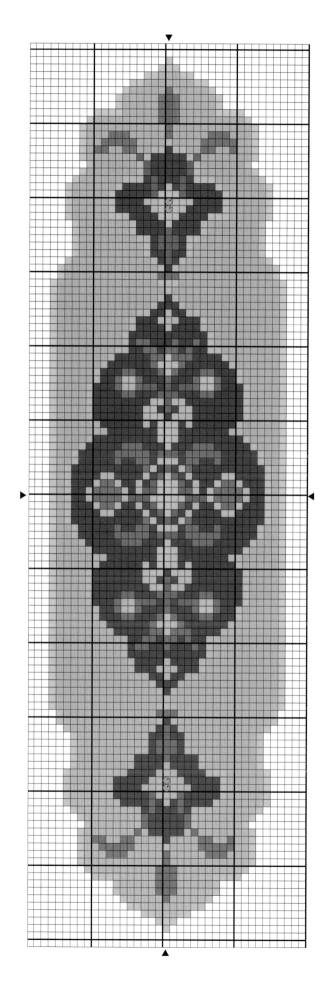

To work the design

Fabric count: 28-count Jobelan or Brittney worked over 2 threads to give 14-count

Number of strands: 2 unless otherwise indicated

Stitch count: 33 x 118

Design size: 2⁴⁄₁₀ x 8⁴⁄₁₀in (6 x 21.4cm)

Thread required

	46
	280
	Lamé 300 Gold†
	123
	843
	Mill Hill beads: Glass Seed 02011

†Use 3 strands

Cream Beaded Border Sampler

This is a most unusual, but beautiful, sampler, which is pleasing to stitch and provides a real sense of achievement upon completion.

During a browsing session in an Indian textile shop, I noticed some exquisite,

heavily beaded cream and white lace in a glass case, which I am told is used for weddings. This sampler is based on my memory of that lace. Each of the seven borders can be used individually and repeated to any length. I think it would

Materials required

Fabric: 28-count denim blue Jobelan
16 x 21in (41 x 51cm)

Threads:
Anchor Stranded Cotton:
3 skeins of 1302
1 skein of 892, 386
Anchor Perlé 8: 1 ball 386

Beads:
Mill Hill: Antique Glass Seed 03021 x 190,
Petite Glass 40123 x 375
Pearl Beads x 70
Droplet Beads x 15

To work the design

Fabric count: 28-count denim blue Jobelan
worked over 2 threads to give 14-count

Number of strands: 2 of Stranded Cotton,
whole thread of Perlé and 1 strand for
backstitch

Stitch count: 131 x 192

Design size: 9⁹⁄₁₀ x 13⁷⁄₁₀in (23.8 x 34.8cm)

Thread required

	892
	386
	386 Perlé 8
	1302 Variegated thread
	Mill Hill beads Antique Glass Seed 03021
	Pearl beads
	Droplet beads
	Mill Hill beads: Petite Glass 40123
	386 x 1*
	Perlé 386*

*Backstitch

make a wonderful wedding sampler if the date of the wedding and the initials of the bride and groom were included. Alternatively, small sections could be adapted for a card.

I used some Mill Hill beads, but also included a few pearl and droplet beads. Beads are readily available in a variety of styles, so you could adapt the design and use white or cream beads of your choice.

Working the design

First edge the fabric to prevent fraying. I recommend that you work it in a rectangular frame, as it provides a more stable base on which to fasten the beads. Stitch the design in the centre of the fabric. Then complete each pattern of beads. Use a needle-threader to help thread a beading needle with a single strand of cream cotton. Making sure that the beginning is secure, fasten each bead with a diagonal stitch like the first 'arm' of a cross stitch and fasten off the thread firmly.

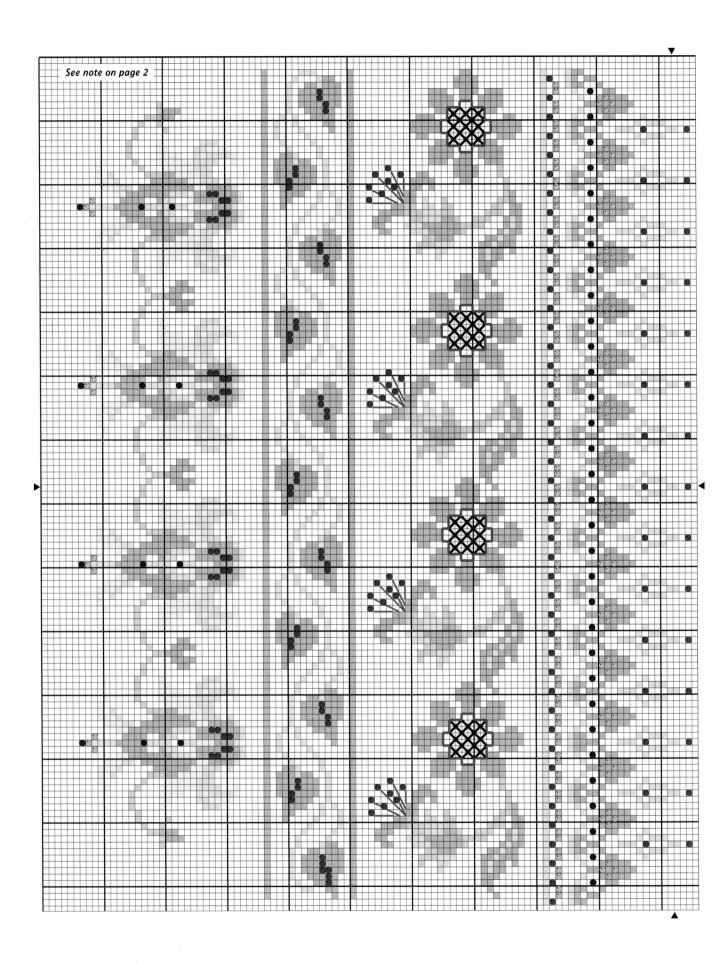

See note on page 2

Cross-Stitch Designs from India

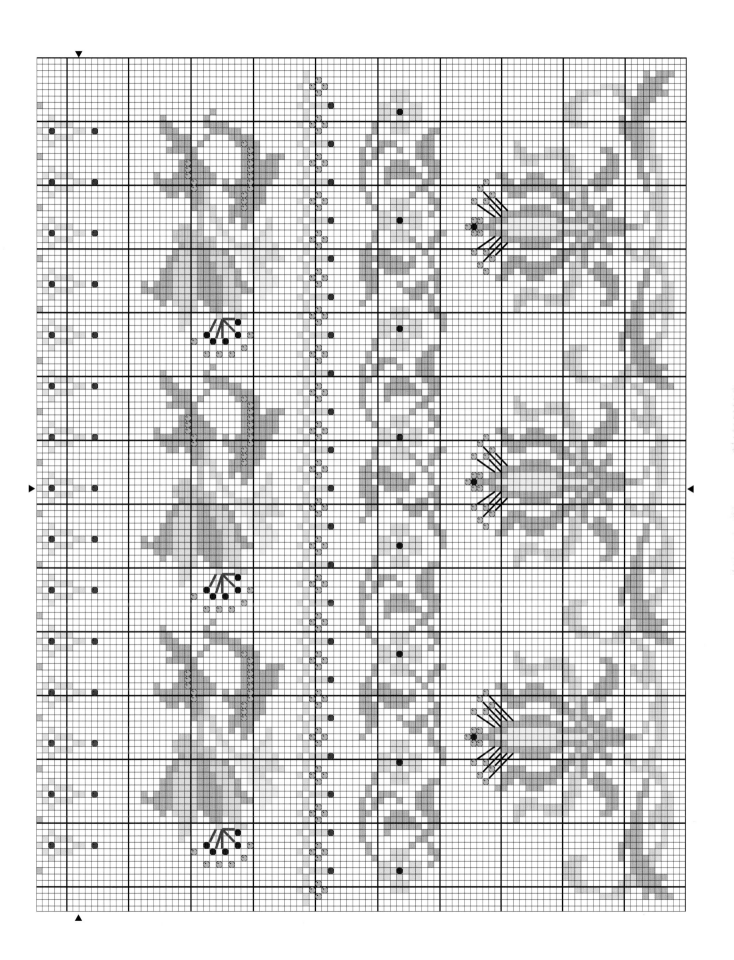

Evening Bag Design

Working the design

First edge the fabric, then stitch the design in the centre widthways, but with the bottom starting 3in (8.5cm) from the edge. Use one strand of cotton, two strands of lamé for the flowers and one strand of lamé for the backstitch to give a delicate design. Cut a piece of Vilene 7 x 23in (18 x 59cm) and iron it in the centre of the fabric. Then turn the end without the stitching onto the right side for 8in (20.5cm) and machine-

I love the small bags from India that are embroidered with gold, so I looked for a design that could be adapted in this style for an evening bag. Eventually I found this one, which is taken from a fragment of a much larger piece of embroidery. As black is always suitable for evening wear, I used 28-count black Jobelan stitched over two threads, with only one strand of cotton and two of lamé, and a piece of fabric 8 x 23in (21 x 59cm) that was large enough to make up into the actual bag.

A few beads, two shiny gold tassels and a gold cord handle provide interest but do not detract from the stitching. I lined the bag with fine red and gold cotton and added a velcro fastening.

To work the design

Fabric count: 28-count black Jobelan or Brittney worked over 2 threads to give 14-count

Number of strands: 1 except gold cross stitch which is 2

Stitch count: 87 x 82

Design size: 6²⁄₁₀ x 5⁹⁄₁₀in (15.8 x 14.9cm)

Materials required

Fabric: 28-count black Jobelan or Brittney 8 x 23in (21 x 59cm)

Threads:
Anchor Stranded Cotton: small amounts of 326, 46, 47, 316
Anchor Lamé: small amount 303 gold
Anchor Marlitt: small amount 850

Beads:
Mill Hill: Glass Seed 02011 x 38

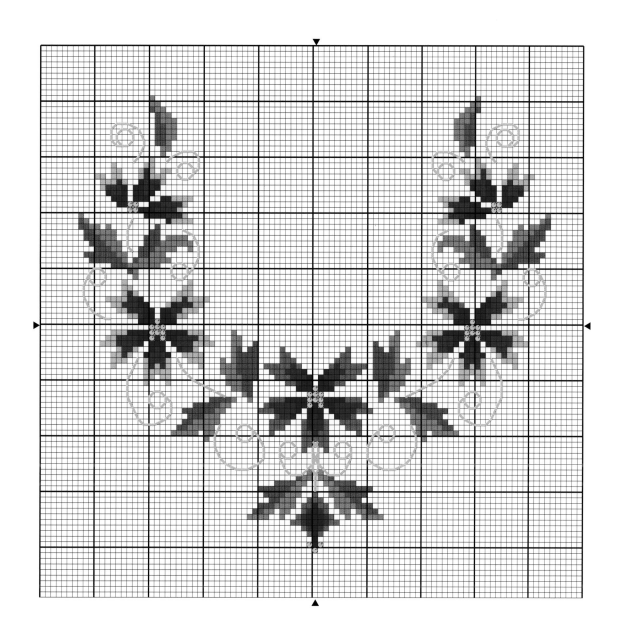

stitch the side seams. Turn the bag part through to the right side. You will now have a bag and the stitching should fold forward to form the front flap. Turn in a small hem all the way round, shaping the flap if you wish. Cut a piece of backing fabric, such as cotton, the same size as the Jobelan. With right sides together, fold one end over 8in (20.5cm) and machine-stitch the side seams. This forms the lining for the bag and needs to be slip-stitched all the way round. Add a handle, beads or tassels as you wish.

Thread required

	326
	47
	46
	Marlitt 850
	Lamé 303 Gold
	316
	Mill Hill beads Glass Seed 02011
	Lamé 303 Gold*

*Backstitch

Designs from Art and Travelling Theatre

Akbar the Great came to rule in 1556. He had been in exile in Persia with Humayun, whose tomb forms the basis of the project on pages 125–127. During their time in exile, Humayun and Akbar became interested in drawing and painting. Humayun asked two Persian artists to arrange a royal workshop in Agra as soon as he was reinstated, but he died after only a year by falling from his library steps. Akbar continued and developed the workshop to become the Mughal School of Painting.

The popularity of painting increased throughout the time of Jahangir and Shah Jahan, and this left a legacy of superb studies of plants, flowers, animals and birds, of which some are now extinct. Often the most beautiful borders surrounded the paintings, and it is these that inspired the floral designs within this chapter.

Many of the colours used in art have symbolic meanings in India. Indigo or blue signifies Krishna, who is one of the representatives of the god Vishnu, and is also the colour worn by a woman for a night-time assignation with her lover. Red signifies love, too, which is the reason brides wear this colour to their weddings – it signifies marital harmony. The more intense the colour, the stronger the love. Madder represents the truest form of love because it cannot be washed out. Yellow, representing corn, mangoes, mustard and the harvest, stands for fertility. Saffron signifies martyrdom and white stands for purity and is the colour of Shiva, the great Hindu god.

Paintings play a role in travelling theatre, too. Travelling bards (called bhopas), or storytellers, used to have hand-painted cotton backdrops or storyboards called 'phads', which they rolled up on two bamboo ends to carry round with them to illustrate their stories. The tradition of storytelling continues today, but the phads are now machine printed, except for the eyes, which are carefully hand-painted by the storyteller afterwards.

Stories and myths told by these bards originate from two main sources. Many of the stories are from a collection of tales called the 'Pacantantra'. These are fictional stories with a moral lesson. They have been adopted, with only slight changes, by many other countries around the world. One example of these is the story of The Bird Who Overcame the Ocean.

A small bird built his nest on the ocean shore despite his wife protesting that it would be swept away by the waves. The bird said they were safe because the ocean was his friend, but the next day the ocean washed away their nest containing eggs and the wife was upset. However, her husband said he would gather together all the birds and they would peck all the water from the ocean and recover the nest. When he told this to the ocean, it just laughed because it was so big.

The birds decided to ask for help from the king of birds, Garuda. Garuda sent a messenger to the god Vishnu to say that the ocean had stolen his servant's eggs. When he heard this, Vishnu became very angry and threatened to dry up the ocean. At this point, the frightened ocean returned the eggs safe and sound to their nest. The moral of this story is that God will help those who help themselves.

The other main source of the stories is the Jataka stories which consist of 547 tales told by Buddha and written down around 400 BC. These tell mainly of Buddha's life and the many births of Buddha in his animal and human lives. In each birth he performed a wonderful deed that took him further along the spiritual path, and it is these acts that are told as stories which also provide teaching and guidance for the buddhists in the villages visited by the bards.

Afghan Wall-Hanging

Cross-Stitch Designs from India

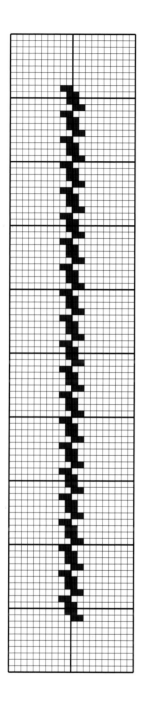

This was stitched over every thread using two strands of cotton and three strands of lamé on 18-count Afghan fabric, but you could stitch it on evenweave fabric and add cross-stitch edges to the border using soft cotton. The designs could be stitched in a vertical line to form a bell-pull. As each individual design uses only a small amount of thread, and the colours are repeated, I have not specified an exact amount; one skein will suffice for several designs.

Working the design

Overcast the edges to prevent fraying, then stitch a design in the centre of each square and a border in the centre of each border 'gap' using two strands of cotton and three of lamé working over every thread. When the stitching is complete, turn in the side and bottom edges leaving a small border, then turn in the top, leaving 1⁴⁄₁₀in (3cm). I filled in the outside intersection squares and stitched a sequin flower pearl to the central ones, then fastened two matching sequin pearls to the tabs.

I hung the design on a piece of three-quarter-inch dowelling with two wooden cabinet handles glued on the ends, but it could also be hung with a bamboo pole or a rod, using small tabs, as I have done, or wooden curtain rings. If you want to make the back neater and give the hanging extra weight, slip-stitch a light-coloured lining to the four edges.

✤ To work the design

✤ **Fabric count:** 18-count Afghan worked over every thread

✤ **Number of strands:** 2

Afghan Flower 1

Materials required
Fabric: 18-count Afghan fabric

Threads:
Anchor Stranded Cotton: 403, 5975, 338, 9, 386, 843, 269, 268, 266
Anchor Lamé: gold 300

To work the design
Stitch count: 70 x 81

Design size: 3⁹⁄₁₀ x 4⁵⁄₁₀in (9.9 x 11.4cm)

Thread required

■	403
■	5975
■	338/5975
▨	9
□	386/9
▨	843
■	269
■	269/268
■	268
■	266
■	268/266
▬	Lamé 300 Gold*†

*Backstitch †Use 3 strands

Afghan Flower 2

Materials required

Fabric: 18-count Afghan fabric

Threads:
Anchor Stranded Cotton: 843, 269, 268, 334, 46, 332
Anchor Lamé: gold 300

To work the design

Stitch count: 60 x 81

Design size: 3³⁄₁₀ x 4⁵⁄₁₀in (8.5 x 11.4cm)

Thread required

	Lamé 300 Gold†
	843
	269
	269/268
	268
	334
	46/334
	332/334
	Lamé 300 Gold*†

*Backstitch   †Use 3 strands

Afghan Flower 3

Materials required

Fabric: 18-count Afghan fabric

Threads:
Anchor Stranded Cotton: 403, 269, 843, 268, 266, 69, 76, 74
Anchor Lamé: gold 300

To work the design

Stitch count: 60 x 80

Design size: 3³⁄₁₀ x 4⁴⁄₁₀in (8.5 x 11.3cm)

Thread required

■	403
	Lamé 300 Gold†
	843
	269
	268/266
	268
	266
	69
	69/76
	76
	74/76
	Lamé 300 Gold*†

*Backstitch   †Use 3 strands

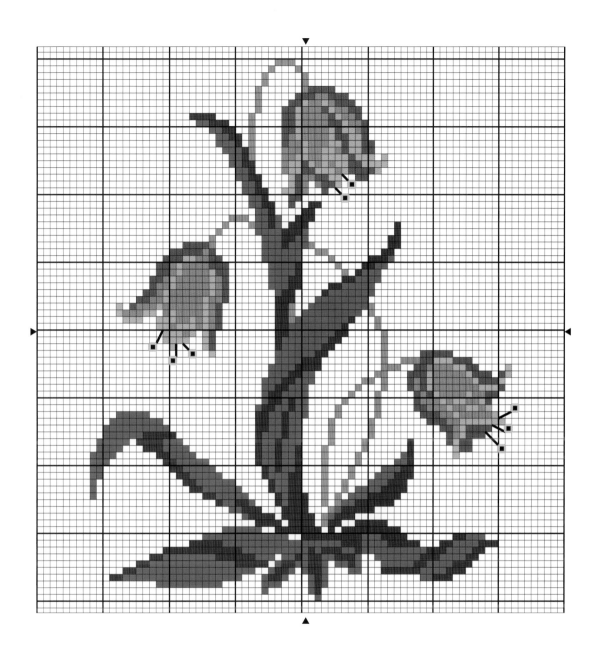

Afghan Flower 4

Materials required

Fabric: 18-count Afghan fabric

Threads:
Anchor Stranded Cotton: 403, 843, 269, 268, 266, 326, 316, 307
Anchor Lamé: gold 300

To work the design

Stitch count: 65 x 80

Design size: 3⁶⁄₁₀ x 4⁴⁄₁₀in (9.2 x 11.3cm)

Thread required

	403
	843
	269
	268/266
	268
	326
	316/326
	316/307
	307
	Lamé 300 Gold*†
	403*

*Backstitch †Use 3 strands

Afghan Flower 5

Materials required

Fabric: 18-count Afghan fabric

Threads:
Anchor Stranded Cotton: 403, 843, 269, 268, 266, 108, 109, 110, 112, 386
Anchor Lamé: gold 300

To work the design

Stitch count: 72 x 81

Design size: 4 x 4⁵⁄₁₀in (10.2 x 11.4cm)

Thread required

■	403
	Lamé 300 Gold†
	843
	269
	269/268
	268
	266
	108
	109/110
	110
	112/110
	386/108
—	Lamé 300 Gold*†

*Backstitch †Use 3 strands

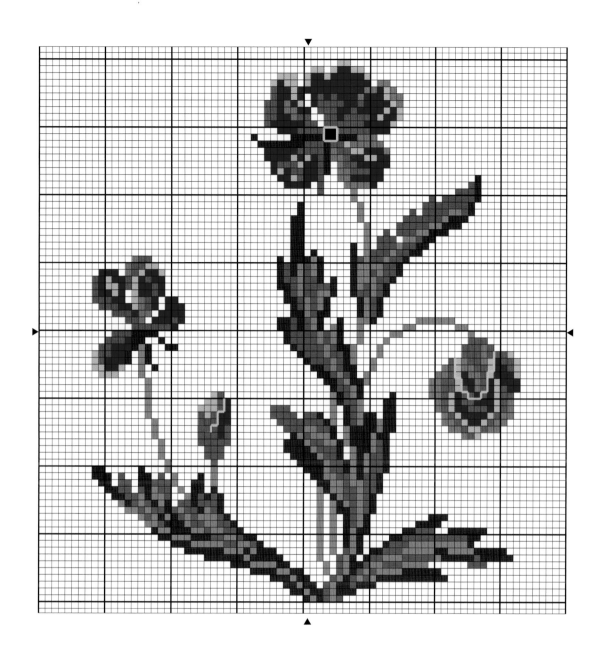

Afghan Flower 6

Materials required

Fabric: 18-count Afghan fabric

Threads:
Anchor Stranded Cotton: 403, 843, 269, 268, 266, 46, 332, 334, 326
Anchor Lamé: gold 300

To work the design

Stitch count: 65 x 80

Design size: 3⁹⁄₁₀ x 4⁴⁄₁₀in (9.2 x 11.3cm)

Thread required

■	403
	843
	269
	268
	268/266
	46
	332/334
	334/326
	326/46
	Lamé 300 Gold*†

*Backstitch †Use 3 strands

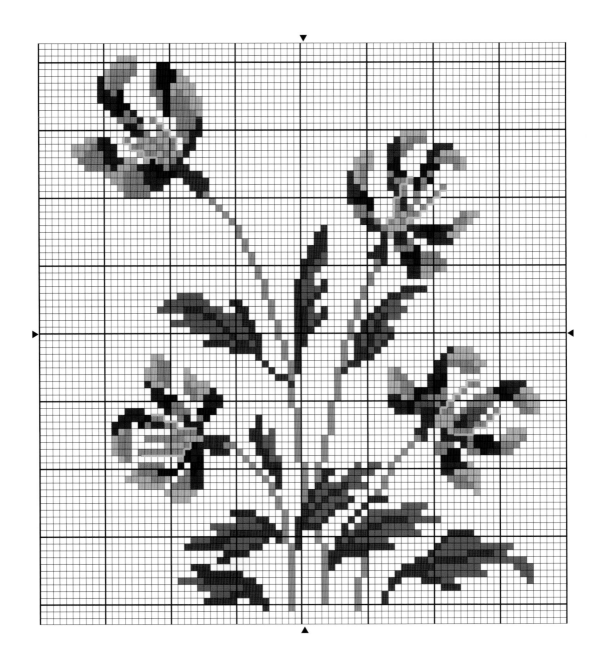

Afghan Flower 7

Materials required

Fabric: 18-count Afghan fabric

Threads:
Anchor Stranded Cotton: 843, 269, 268, 266, 307, 108, 110, 112
Anchor Lamé: gold 300

To work the design

Stitch count: 71 x 82

Design size: 3⁹⁄₁₀ x 4⁶⁄₁₀in (10 x 11.6cm)

Thread required

	843
	269
	268
	268/266
	307
	108
	108/110
	110
	112/110
	112
	Lamé 300 Gold*†

*Backstitch †Use 3 strands

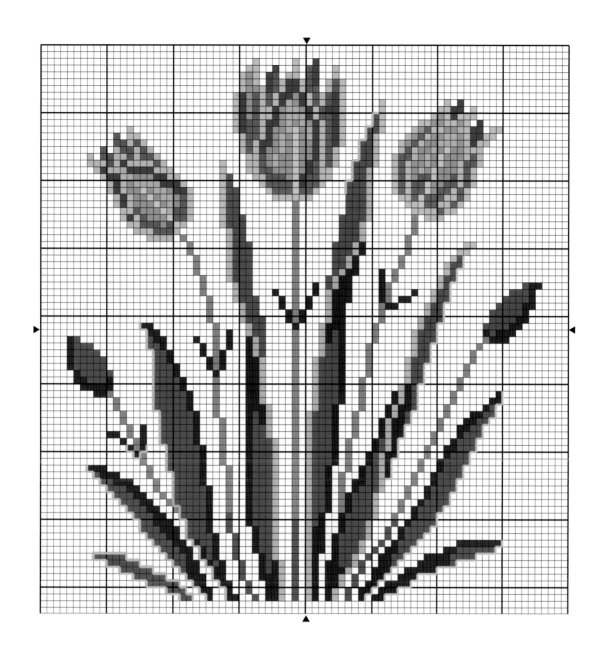

Afghan Flower 8

Materials required

Fabric: 18-count Afghan fabric

Threads:
Anchor Stranded Cotton: 843, 269, 268, 334, 332, 330, 326, 266
Anchor Lamé: gold 300

To work the design

Stitch count: 72 x 80

Design size: 4 x 4⁴⁄₁₀in (10.2 x 11.3cm)

Thread required

	Lamé 300 Gold†
	843
	269
	266/268
	268
	334
	332/334
	330/332
	334/326
	330
	Lamé 301 Gold*†

*Backstitch †Use 3 strands

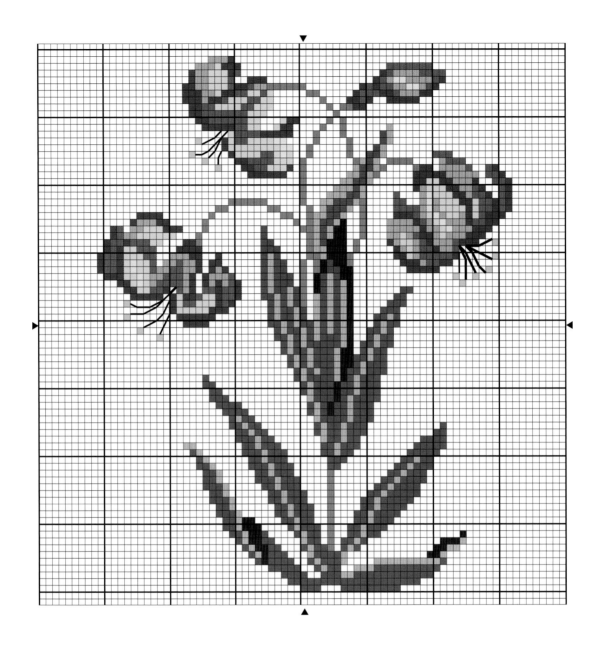

Afghan Flower 9

Materials required

Fabric: 18-count Afghan fabric

Threads:
Anchor Stranded Cotton: 403, 843, 269, 268, 266, 69, 76, 75, 74
Anchor Lamé: gold 300

To work the design

Stitch count: 63 x 79

Design size: 3⁵⁄₁₀ x 4⁴⁄₁₀in (8.9 x 11.1cm)

Thread required

	Lamé 300 Gold†
	843
	269
	268
	268/266
	266
	69
	69/76
	76
	74/76
	75
	403*

*Backstitch   †Use 3 strands

Afghan Decorative Cushions

These three designs match the designs in the wall-hanging above, so the twelve designs are interchangeable. They are adapted from margin borders from the early seventeenth century. I have made them into small decorative cushions that have cream backs and tassels at the corners. A pearl flower sequin and a pink bead that matches the stitched flower hide the fastenings.

Working the designs

Each design needs to be one complete square of 18-count Afghan fabric with a half-square border on all four sides. Overcast the edges to prevent fraying, then stitch the design in the centre of the square, working over every thread using two strands of cotton and three strands of lamé. Make the 2¾in (7cm) tassels from cream wool (Anchor Tapisserie 8002) using thirty-two wraps over a 3in (8cm) piece of card.

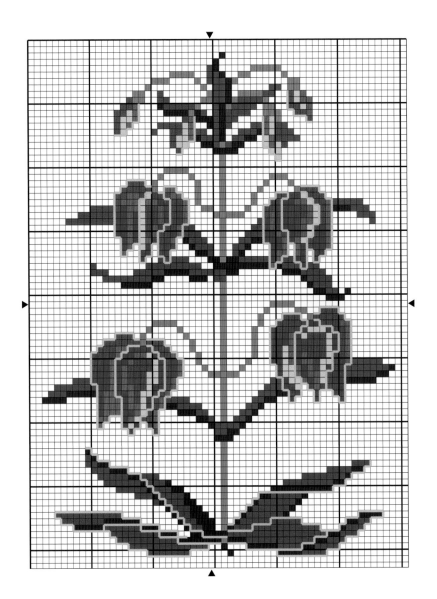

Afghan Flower 10

Materials required

Fabric: One 18-count Afghan square with border

Threads:
Anchor Stranded Cotton: 1 skein 268, 269, 334, small amounts of 843, 326, 330
Anchor Lamé: small amount gold 303

To work the design

Fabric count: One 18-count Afghan square with border

Number of strands: 2 of cotton, 3 of Lamé

Stitch count: 57 x 79

Design size: 3²⁄₁₀ x 4⁴⁄₁₀in (8 x 11.1cm)

Thread required

	843
	269
	269/268
	268
	334
	326
	334/326
	330/334
	Lamé 303 Gold*†

*Backstitch †Use 3 strands

Afghan Flower 11

Thread required

	Lamé 303 Gold†
	843
	269
	269/268
	268
	69
	69/76
	76
	74/76
	307
	74/894
	1028
	Lamé 303 Gold*†

*Backstitch   †Use 3 strands

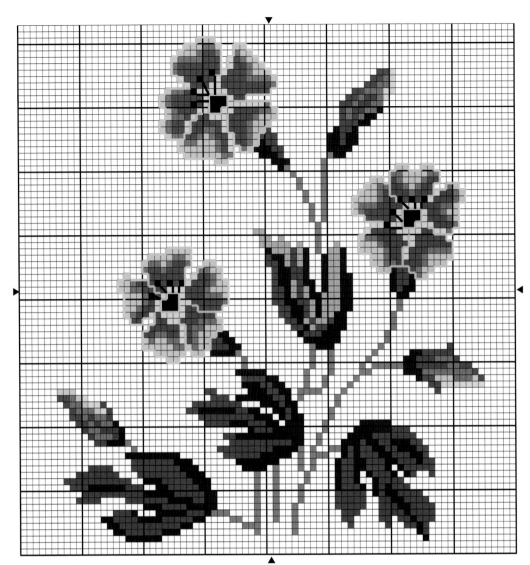

Afghan Flower 12

Materials required

Fabric: One 18-count Afghan square with border

Threads:
Anchor Stranded Cotton: 1 skein 268, 269, 338, small amounts of 403, 5975, 9, 843, 266
Anchor Lamé: small amount gold 303

To work the design

Fabric count: One 18-count Afghan square with border

Number of strands: 2 of cotton, 3 of Lamé

Stitch count: 69 x 79

Design size: 3⁸⁄₁₀ x 4⁴⁄₁₀in (9.7 x 11.1cm)

Thread required

■	403
▨	338/5975
▨	338/9
▨	843
■	269
▨	269/268
▨	268
▨	266
▨	9
▨	338
—	Lamé 303 Gold*†
▬	403*

*Backstitch   †Use 3 strands

Mughal Flower Designs

These designs are all adaptations of a late seventeenth-/early eighteenth-century border that is in the British Museum. The reds and oranges are particularly striking, and to show them to their best effect I have stitched the picture on black fabric. However, as some people do not like working on dark fabric, I have worked the pot-pourri cushion on a paler fabric. Stitching the smaller card is an enjoyable way to use up the threads.

Picture
Working the design

If working on black fabric I'd advise you to either work in daylight or use a spotlight at night so that you can see the stitches. Orange and red look quite dramatic on dark fabric, so I have allowed a wide mount and border to enable the picture to stand out, rather than being dominated by the frame. If you would like your picture to be smaller, though, simply use a smaller piece of fabric. Overcast the edges to prevent fraying, then stitch the design in the centre using two strands of cotton and three strands of lamé over two threads.

Materials required

Fabric: 28-count black Jobelan or Brittney 20 x 19in (51 x 48.5cm)

Threads:
Anchor Stranded Cotton: 2 skeins 245, 1 skein 330, 334, 42, 205, 306, 41, 55, 46, 1044, small amounts of 403, 1, 40
Anchor Lamé: gold 303

To work the design

Fabric count: 28-count black Jobelan or Brittney worked over 2 threads to give 14-count

Number of strands: 2 of cotton, 3 of Lamé

Stitch count: 127 x 118

Design size: 9¹⁄₁₀ x 8⁴⁄₁₀in (23 x 21.4cm)

Thread required

■	403		▨	205
□	1 on black, 386 on white		▨	245/306
▨	330		▨	41
▨	334		▨	55
▨	46		▨	Lamé 303 Gold†
▨	245		━	46*
▨	40		━	42*
▨	42		━	1044*

*Backstitch   †Use 3 strands

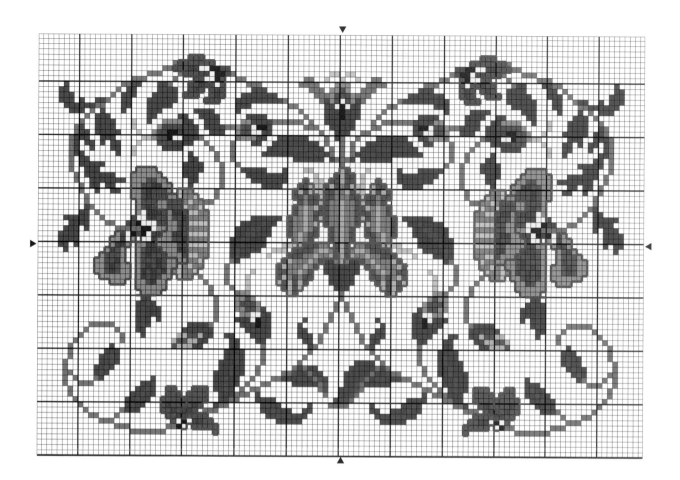

Pot-Pourri Cushion
Working the design

This is worked over every thread on 19-count Easistitch. Edge the fabric to stop fraying, then stitch the design in the centre using two strands of cotton and three strands of lamé. Use a green velvet back and add a ready-made dark green and gold tassel at the bottom left-hand corner to finish it off.

Materials required
Fabric: 19-count fabric 10 x 8in
(25.5 x 20cm)

Threads:
Anchor Stranded Cotton: 1 skein 330, 334, 245, 205, 306, 41
small amounts of 403, 1, 46, 42, 55
Anchor Lamé: gold 303

To work the design
Fabric count: 19-count over every thread
Number of strands: 2 of cotton, 3 of Lamé
Stitch count: 103 x 71
Design size: 7⁸⁄₁₀ x 5¹⁄₁₀in (19.8 x 13.9cm)

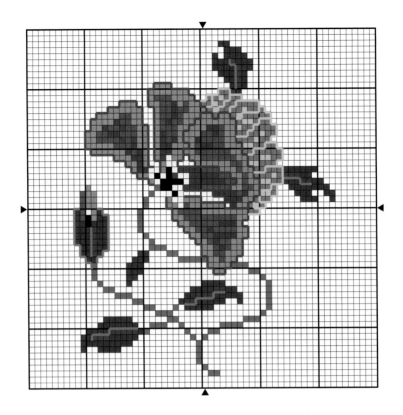

Card
Working the design

First work the stitches, then, when they are complete, iron a piece of Vilene on the back, and fasten it to a cream card from Framecraft with an aperture of 5½ x 3¾in (13.9 x 9.5cm).

Materials required

Fabric: 28-count Jobelan or Brittney
4³⁄₁₀ x 5²⁄₁₀in (11 x 13cm)

Threads:
Anchor Stranded Cotton: 1 skein 330,
small amounts of 403, 386, 334, 46, 245, 205,
306, 41, 42, 1044
Anchor Lamé: gold 303

To work the design

Fabric count: 28-count Jobelan or Brittney
worked over 2 threads to give
14-count

Number of strands: 2 of cotton, 3 of Lamé

Stitch count: 45 x 56

Design size: 3²⁄₁₀ x 4in (8.2 x 10.2cm)

Indian Flower Picture

A painting in the British Museum inspired this design. It has been simplified to make it practical to stitch, but the muted pink and gold border does manage to convey the same impression as the original.

Part of the design has been stitched using De Haviland variegated thread, but it could be replaced with Anchor stranded cotton. Use one strand each of 63 and 65 as a substitute for the pink and 98 and 100 for the purple.

Working the design

Overcast the edges to prevent fraying, then work the design in the centre of the fabric using two strands of cotton and three strands of lamé over two threads.

Materials required

Fabric: 28-count ivory Jobelan or Brittney 15 x 10in (38 x 25.5cm)

Threads:
Anchor Stranded Cotton: 3 skeins 1019, 1 skein 246
De Haviland variegated thread: 1 skein pink, purple or Anchor Stranded Cotton: 1 skein 63, 65, 98, 100
Anchor Lamé: 1 skein 300

To work the design

Fabric count: 28-count ivory Jobelan or Brittney worked over 2 threads to give 14-count

Number of strands: 2 of cotton, 3 of Lamé

Stitch count: 156 x 86

Design size: $11\frac{1}{10}$ x $6\frac{1}{10}$in (28.3 x 15.6cm)

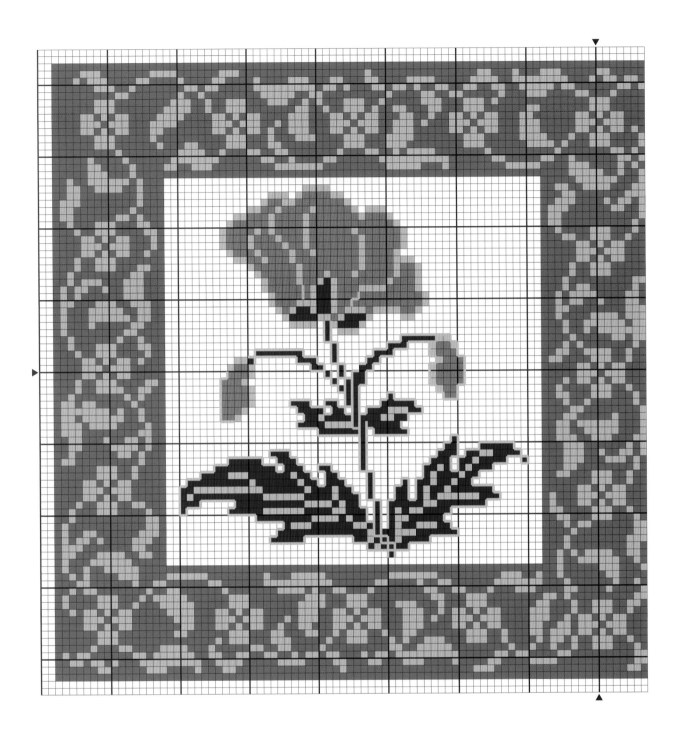

Thread required

▨	1019
▨	Lamé 300 Gold
▨	246
▨	De Haviland pink
▨	De Haviland purple
▨	Lamé 300 Gold*

*Backstitch

Cross-Stitch Designs from India

See note on page 2

Ganesha Cushion

Shiva is one of the great Hindu gods and
Ganesha is his orange, elephant-headed,
pot-bellied son. He is the remover of
obstacles to happiness and satisfaction and
has custody of doorways. Consequently,
businesses and new undertakings call upon
Ganesha to help them overcome any
problems, and door-hangings often picture
him. He is characteristically shown with a
stick, a goad, his rat companion and a
noose or necklace, and usually has a bowl
of sweetmeats.

Working the design

Work the design in the centre of the canvas
using tent stitch for the main picture and
background, cross stitch for the purple and

See note on page 2

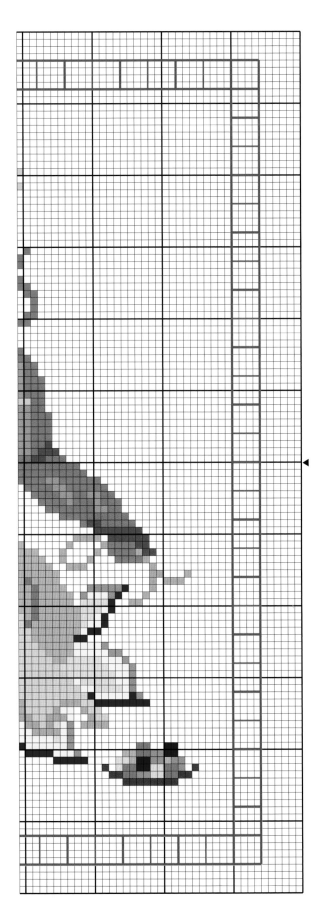

gold necklaces, and a border of Rhodes stitch. The diagonal lines represent the first stitch of each Rhodes stitch.

To complete the cushion, make two large black tassels using stranded cotton. Then stitch smaller tassels in cream and burgundy around the edges. Finally, stitch the large tassels at the two top corners of the cushion and cover their fastenings with silver shisha mirrors.

Note

The background has been left clear to make it easier to follow the chart. It should in fact be black.

Thread required

	9800
	8196
	8192
	8198
	8036
	8718
	9192
	9198
	8104
	Lamé 303 Gold†
	8424
	8002
	8398
	8734
	8732
	8596
———	Shows direction of first stitch for Rhodes*
———	Shows Rhodes stitches*

*Backstitch   †Use 6 strands

Matching Flower Pictures

These flowers are derived from Mughal painted borders from the early seventeenth century. They are straightforward to work and fairly quick to complete. Although they are not identical in colour, they are similar enough to make a matching pair.

I allowed much more fabric than usual to cater for the wide mount I had chosen. While I was stitching them I had a scrap piece of fabric tucked under the frame clips to help them to grip. Coincidentally, it formed a sort of border that really set the pictures off, so I decided to use this idea in the finished work. I fastened strips of folded fabric, made firm with Vilene, between the mount and the stitching. In my collection of cotton materials, I was lucky to find this red, gold and orange piece that was just right.

Materials required for picture 1

Fabric: 26-count linen 14 x 17in (35.5 x 43cm) to allow for the mount

Threads:
Anchor Stranded Cotton: 1 skein of 11, 1025, 266, 268, 269, 1014, small amounts of 1, 3 86, 361
Anchor Lamé: small amount gold 303

Materials required for picture 2

Fabric: 26-count linen 14 x 17in (35.5 x 43cm) to allow for wide mount

Threads:
Anchor Stranded Cotton: 1 skein of 266, 268, small amounts of 972, 970, 969, 340, 332, 269
Anchor Lamé: small amount gold 303

Beads:
Mill Hill: Petite Glass 40557 x 18

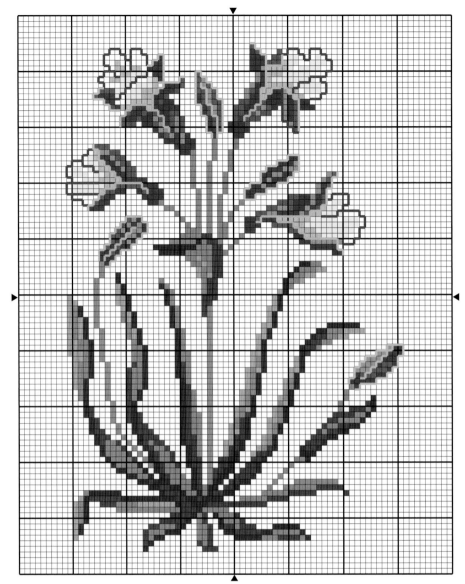

Picture 1

Working the designs

Overcast the edges to prevent fraying, then stitch the pictures in the centre of the fabric using two strands of cotton and three strands of lamé over two threads. Outline and add beads.

Thread required

	1
	386
	361
	11/1025
	11
	1025
	1014/1025
	266
	268
	269/268
	266/white
	1014*
	Lamé 303 Gold*†

*Backstitch †Use 3 strands

To work the design

Fabric count: 26-count linen worked over 2 threads

Number of strands: 2 of cotton, 3 of Lamé

Stitch count: 62 x 91

Design size: 4⁸⁄₁₀ x 7in (12.1 x 17.8cm)

Picture 2

To work the design

Fabric count: 26-count linen worked over 2 threads

Number of strands: 2 of cotton, 3 of Lamé

Stitch count: 63 x 89

Design size: 4⁸⁄₁₀ x 6⁸⁄₁₀in (12.3 x 17.4cm)

Thread required

■	972
■	970/972
■	969
■	340
■	340/332
■	332
■	269
■	269/268
■	268
■	266/268
■	Mill Hill beads Petite Glass 40557
─	Lamé 303 Gold*†

*Backstitch   †Use 3 strands

Indian Ladies Picture

Materials required

Fabric: 28-count Jobelan 22 x 18in
(56 x 46cm)

Threads:
Anchor Stranded Cotton: 3 skeins of 1012,
9575, 1 skein of 403, 70, 1013, 131, 130, 85,
small amounts of 1, 400, 87, 1027, 86, 1089
Anchor Lamé: 303, 300, 301

Beads:
Mill Hill: Glass Seed 02011 x 57,
Petite Glass 40557 x 67

To work the design

Fabric count: 28-count dark blue Jobelan
or Brittney worked over 2 threads to give
14-count

Number of strands: 2 of cotton, 3 of Lamé

Stitch count: 219 x 143

Design size: 15⁵⁄₁₀ x 10²⁄₁₀in (39.7 x 25.9cm)

This picture is quite a large undertaking as
there is a lot of stitching, so I wouldn't
recommend it to a beginner. However,
I found it well worth the effort and it makes
a striking picture when hung on the wall.

It is adapted from a storyboard, or 'phad'
as they are known, that storytellers carry to
help illustrate their tales. Faces on many
Indian paintings are identical and it is only
by the form of dress or by different gestures
that individuals can be identified. The phad
from which I adapted this picture was like
this, so the two people are nearly identical.
In fact, the storytellers often used the same
backdrop for a number of stories and just
adjusted the scenery or clothing, so one
face might represent many characters.
For this, it is obviously better to have fairly
expressionless faces.

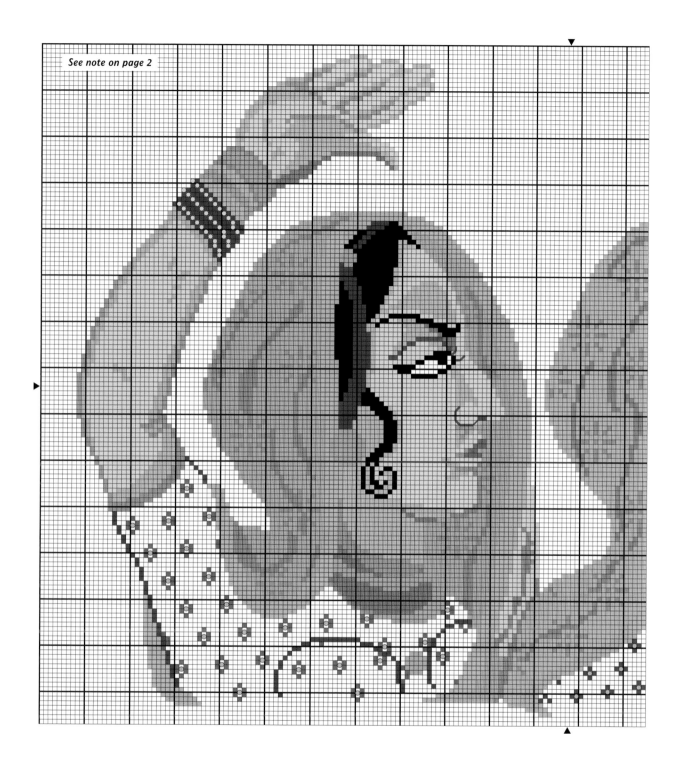

See note on page 2

Working the design

Overcast the edges to prevent fraying, then work the design in the centre of the fabric. Add a small gold bead (Mill Hill Petite Glass 40557) in the centre of each flower on the dresses. Stitch the beads on the wrists (Mill Hill Glass Seed 02011), then the gold necklaces which can be beads, a sequin band or gold braid, then stitch on the decoration above the ears and in the centre of the dresses. The decorations are all optional. If you wish, you could just stitch gold lamé, but I think they add interest and finish off the stitching.

Thread required

■	403		130/silver lamé
	1		85/silver lamé
	70		87
	Lamé 300 Gold†		1027
	Lamé 303/300		Lamé 303 Gold††
	400/1013		86/silver lamé
	1012		1089
	9575		85
	1013/9575		Mill Hill beads Glass Seed 02011
	1012/9575		Mill Hill beads Petite Glass 40557
	131/silver lamé	▬	400*

*Backstitch   †Use 2 strands   ††Use 3 strands

Ornamental Bookmark

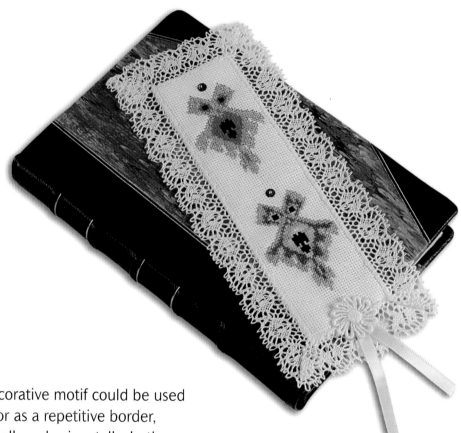

This small decorative motif could be used either singly or as a repetitive border, worked vertically or horizontally. In these colours it makes a vibrant bookmark. Green sequins, fastened by small gold beads, provide the finishing touch. Remember that any embellishments you add to a bookmark must not be bulky as they could damage the pages.

Working the design

Start the design nine threads down from the top of the bookmark. When you have completed the stitching, finish the back off by slip-stitching a length of ribbon down the centre.

Materials required

Fabric: 18-count ivory bookmark from Framecraft

Threads:
Anchor Stranded Cotton: small amounts of 403, 279, 1304, 326, 281
Anchor Lamé: small amount gold 303
Anchor Marlitt: small amount 850

Sequins:
2 x small green

Beads:
Mill Hill: Petite Glass 40557 x 2

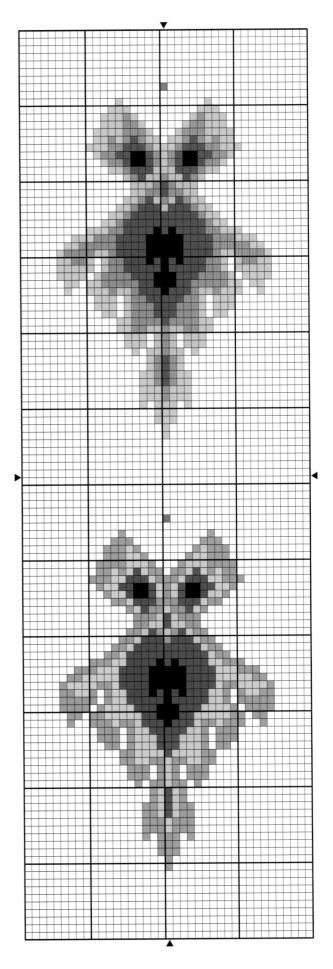

To work the design

Fabric count: 18-count

Number of strands: 2 of cotton, 3 of Lamé

Stitch count: 29 x 104

Design size: 1⁹⁄₁₀ x 5⁸⁄₁₀in (4.1 x 14.7cm)

Thread required

■	403
	279
	Marks position for green sequin
	1304
	326
	Marlitt 850
	Lamé 303 Gold†
	281

†Use 3 strands

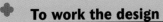

Mehndi Painting Duck Card

Mehndi patterns are used during festivals, and especially for the decoration of brides. Fantastically detailed designs are painstakingly applied to the hands and feet, almost like tattoos, using paint made from henna leaves and water.

Stitched on 22-count over every thread, this Mehndi design will just fit into an aperture of 2in (5cm) square. On 14-count it will fit one of 3in (8cm) square.

Working the design

Work the design in the centre of the fabric, then back with Vilene to give it more strength. To finish, stitch on the gold bead (Mill Hill 40557) or, alternatively, fill in the space using the lamé thread.

Thread required

▨	410
■	152
▨	Lamé 303 Gold†
□	Mill Hill beads Petite Glass 40557 or gold Lamé

†Use 3 strands

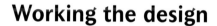

Materials required

Fabric: 22-count linen 3in (8cm) square

Threads:
Anchor Stranded Cotton: small amount 410, 152
Anchor Lamé: small amount gold 303

Beads:
Mill Hill: Petite Glass 40557 x 1

To work the design

Fabric count: 22-count evenweave over every thread

Number of strands: 2 of cotton, 3 of Lamé

Stitch count: 35 x 40

Design size: 1⁹⁄₁₀ x 1⁹⁄₁₀in (4 x 4.6cm)

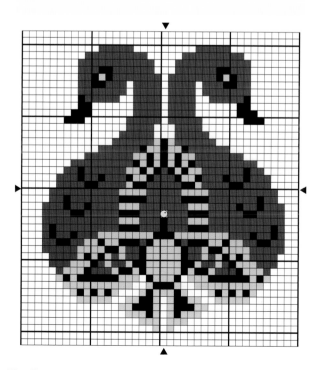

Papier Mâché Design Pincushion

Throughout my exploration of Indian designs, I came across many beautifully decorated bowls and boxes made from papier mâché. This particular design was featured on a papier mâché bowl. However, it was a laquered penbox that inspired my choice of colours.

Worked on 22-count fabric, this design makes a perfect cover for this wooden pincushion, but it has enough detail to be interesting when stitched on a larger count. It would also make a very attractive birthday card.

Working the design

Work the design using three strands of cotton and lamé over every thread, then fill in the background in 386 and extend the worked area to the required size. If you are making a pincushion, measure with a tape measure across the domed top as far as the bottom of the insert, then allow at least 2in (5cm) all the way round for fastening. A stapler can be used to fasten the canvas under the base.

Materials required

Fabric: 22-count light-coloured mono canvas, size to fit your pincushion plus 2in (5cm)

Threads:
Anchor Stranded Cotton: small amounts of 46, 326, 1001, 278, 280, 281, 1304, 306, 307, 846
Cream: 386 sufficient for your background
Anchor Lamé: small amount gold 303

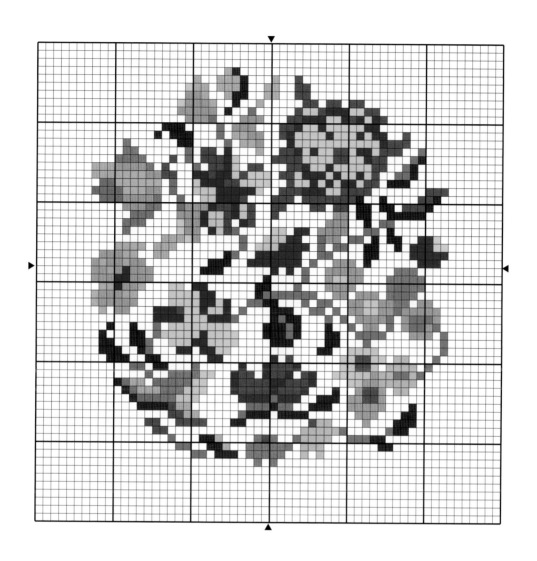

To work the design

Fabric count: 22-count canvas worked over every thread using tent stitch

Number of strands: 3

Stitch count: 46 x 50

Design size: 2¹⁄₁₀ x 2³⁄₁₀in (5.3 x 5.8cm)

Thread required

	46
	326
	1001
	Lamé 303 Gold
	281
	1304
	306
	307
	846
	280
	278

Designs from Architecture

In almost every Indian town and city there are magnificent mosques, temples and monuments. The abundance of these superb-looking buildings inspired me to base the next four designs on them.

The buildings have many similar features, such as domes, tapering walls, beautiful glazed tiles, mirrorwork and carvings. 'Sheesha meenakari' is a particularly beautiful form of interior decoration. It involves attaching a myriad of cut, coloured mirror pieces onto walls and ceilings to create beautiful, reflective, geometric patterns. Palaces and mosques are among the buildings that were decorated by Mughal kings using this technique, and many still remain to be admired today.

Once the pattern has been decided, it is accurately drawn on paper and marked out on the wall or ceiling by a process called 'pouncing'. Small holes are pricked in the paper all round the design. Then, a dusting of blue powder transfers the pattern of holes onto the wall. Using a diamond-nibbed pen, thousands of small pieces of mirror are cut to fit the design and pasted into place. When they are dry, any gaps are grouted with a kind of plaster of Paris mixture.

It is the shape of Indian buildings that fascinates me the most, though, so two of the pictures I have designed are of buildings. As the colours on the exteriors are minimal, I have worked them on dark blue fabric and used a limited palette, but the pictures are enhanced by the use of several different easy-to-work stitches which provides texture.

Please note that it is advisable to use a rectangular or square frame to work these pieces.

Taj Mahal Picture

This design is based on the south façade of the Taj Mahal, which must be one of the most recognizable Mughal structures. It was built in the seventeenth century on the banks of the River Jumna at Agra by the Mughal emperor Shah Jahan in memory of his beloved wife Mumtaz Mahal, who died in childbirth. After a period of mourning, Shah Jahan began to build this mausoleum which took 22 years to complete and gave employment to over 20,000 workers. It is built of ivory-white marble. The only hint of colour comes from the variations in the natural stone.

Working the design

Overcast the edges to prevent fraying, then work the design in the centre of the fabric using the threads and stitches as indicated. If this is your first attempt at these stitches, try them initially on a scrap piece of fabric. The stitches may look intricate but they really are easy. The diagonal line indicates the first Rhodes stitch, then follow the instructions for the stitch given on page 10.

Tip

You will find it easier to work the cross stitches that form the frame for the Rhodes, Scottish and eyelet stitches first, then fill in with the relevant stitches. Note that Rhodes stitch and Scottish stitch are worked in Perlé and eyelet stitch is worked in stranded cotton.

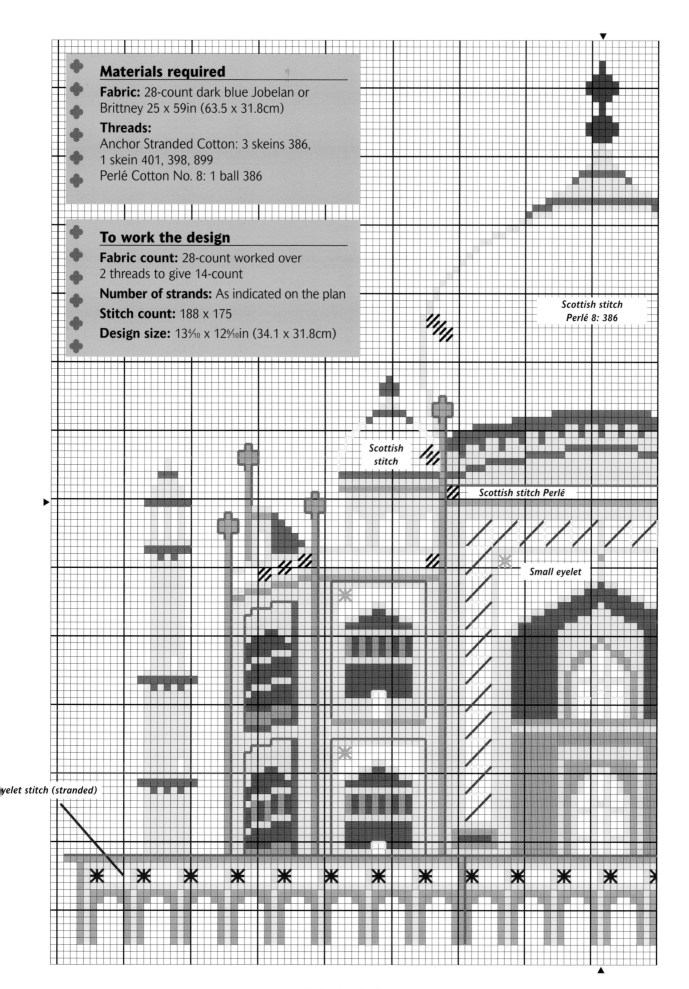

Materials required

Fabric: 28-count dark blue Jobelan or Brittney 25 x 59in (63.5 x 31.8cm)

Threads:
Anchor Stranded Cotton: 3 skeins 386,
1 skein 401, 398, 899
Perlé Cotton No. 8: 1 ball 386

To work the design

Fabric count: 28-count worked over 2 threads to give 14-count

Number of strands: As indicated on the plan

Stitch count: 188 x 175

Design size: 13⁴⁄₁₀ x 12⁶⁄₁₀in (34.1 x 31.8cm)

Scottish stitch
Perlé 8: 386

Scottish stitch

Scottish stitch Perlé

Small eyelet

yelet stitch (stranded)

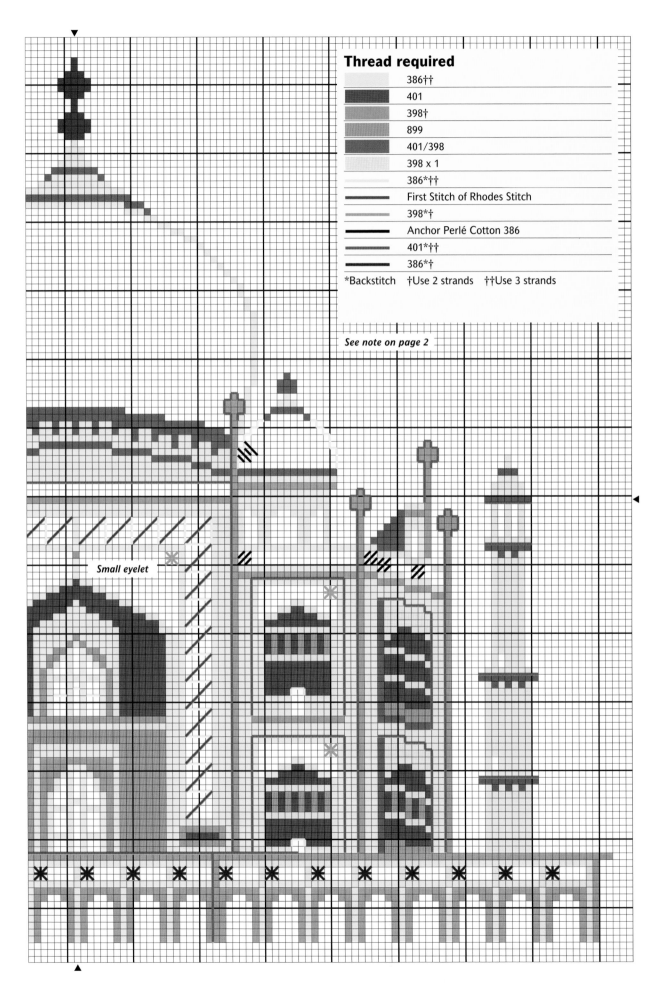

Thread required

	386††
	401
	398†
	899
	401/398
	398 x 1
	386*††
	First Stitch of Rhodes Stitch
	398*†
	Anchor Perlé Cotton 386
	401*††
	386*†

*Backstitch   †Use 2 strands   ††Use 3 strands

See note on page 2

Small eyelet

Cross-Stitch Designs from India

Humayun's Tomb Picture

This picture of Humayun's tomb, completed in 1571 and found in Delhi, would complement the picture of the Taj Mahal shown on page 122, as the tomb was in fact the model for the Taj Mahal.

Babar, the first Mughal ruler, was succeeded by his son Humayun, who was forced to leave India and go into exile in Persia. He regained his throne, but died only a year later, and his widow had the tomb built for him.

Unlike the Taj Mahal, the tomb is made mainly of red sandstone and inlaid with white marble, so I chose tones of burnt sienna, which are particularly effective on the dark blue background.

To work the design follow the same instructions as for the Taj Mahal picture (see page 122).

Materials required

Fabric: 28-count dark blue Jobelan or Brittney 25 x 23in (63.5 x 59cm)

Threads:
Anchor Stranded Cotton: 3 skeins 386, 5975, 2 skeins 914
Perlé Cotton No. 8: 1 ball 386

To work the design

Fabric count: 28-count dark blue Jobelan or Brittney worked over 2 threads to give 14-count

Number of strands: As indicated on the plan

Stitch count: 170 x 134

Design size: 12¹⁄₁₀ x 9⁶⁄₁₀in (30.8 x 24.3cm)

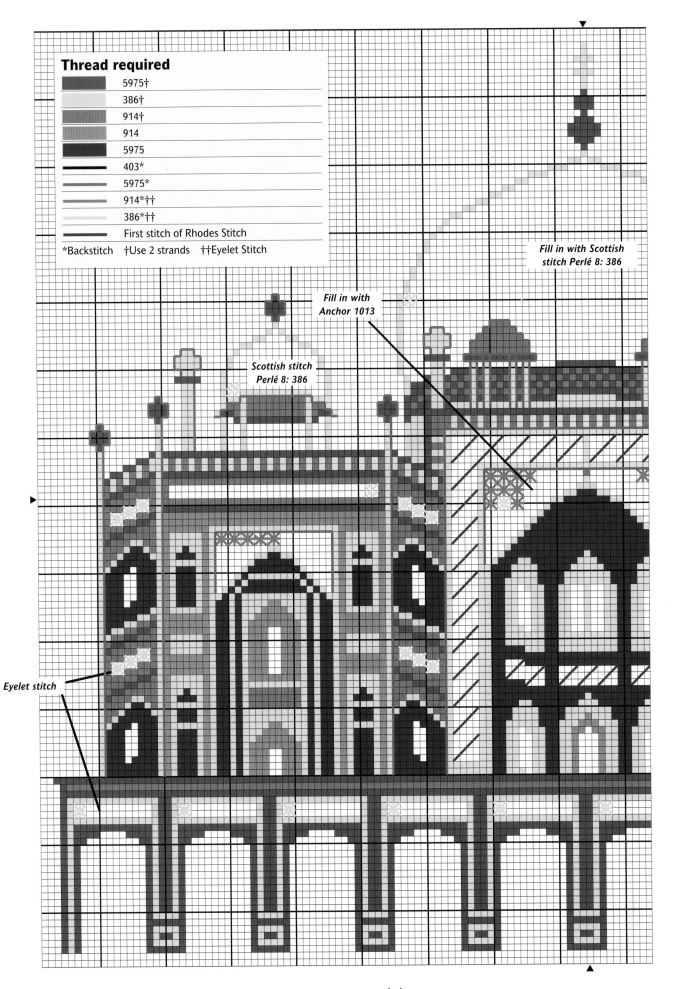

Thread required

	5975†
	386†
	914†
	914
	5975
	403*
	5975*
	914*††
	386*††
	First stitch of Rhodes Stitch

*Backstitch   †Use 2 strands   ††Eyelet Stitch

Fill in with Scottish stitch Perlé 8: 386

Fill in with Anchor 1013

Scottish stitch Perlé 8: 386

Eyelet stitch

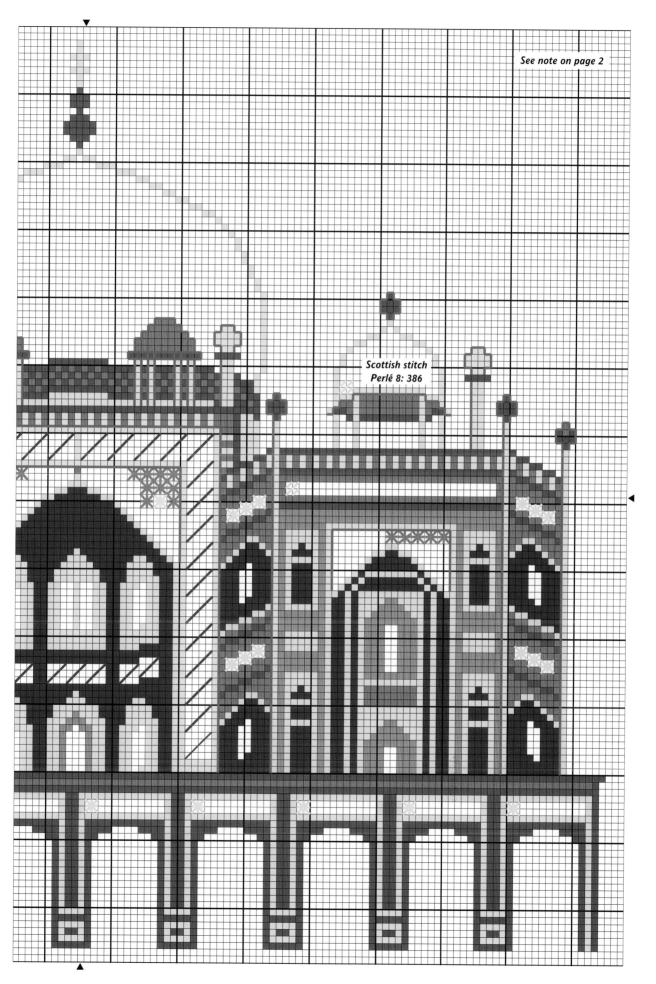

See note on page 2

Scottish stitch
Perlé 8: 386

Taj Mahal
Marble Panel Design

The inspiration for this design came from a beautiful decoration in the Taj Mahal that is carved from white marble and bordered with an inlaid dark marble floral pattern. By working some stitches on top of others and using different types of thread but in the same colour, I have tried to recreate the three-dimensionality of the carving.

The stranded cotton, soft cotton and Coton à Broder used all have different tones and vary according to the changing light. The background and border are worked in half-cross stitch. To give the design maximum impact, the area around the design is left unworked.

The border is stunning on its own, and would make an extremely beautiful frame for a photograph.

Working the design

I recommend that you work this design in a rectangular or square frame. First, start stitching from the centre. Stitch all of the half-cross stitches, then add the long stitches. On the chart there are black dots and blank holes. Each long stitch, which is in Soft Cotton, comes up from the back at the black dots and goes down into the blank holes. As a number of stitches go

Materials required

Fabric: 16-count white mono canvas
13 x 15in (33 x 38cm)

Threads:
Anchor Stranded Cotton: 3 skeins 386, 368
2 skeins 127
1 skein 20
Anchor Coton à Broder: 1 skein 386
Anchor Soft Cotton: 1 skein 386

down into each hole, making them very tight, it may be necessary to gently poke a knitting needle into the holes to open them up a little.

To work the design

Fabric count: 16-count white mono canvas

Number of strands: As indicated on chart

Stitch count: 121 x 145

Design size: 7⁶⁄₁₀ x 9¹⁄₁₀in (19.2 x 23cm)

Thread required

	386 Stranded Cotton††•
	386 Coton à Broder†••
	368††•
	386 Soft Cotton••
	20††•
	127††•
	20 Stranded Cotton†††••
	127†††••
	368†††••
	386 Soft Cotton – long stitches dot to hole
	386 Soft Cotton – long stitches*

*Back stitch †Use 2 strands ††Use 3 strands

†††Use 6 strands •Cross Stitch ••Tent Stitch

Mirrorwork Pot-Pourri Cushion

This design is taken from a fragment of a wall pattern. The pattern was originally in greys and oranges, but I have altered the colours to match the twisted cord.

Working the design

Edge the fabric to prevent fraying, then work the design in the centre using two strands over two threads. If you wish, when you have completed the stitching, iron Vilene onto the back and add some chunky beads to create a greater surface texture.

Materials required

Fabric: 28-count Evenweave 9 x 9in (23 x 23cm)

Threads:
Anchor Stranded Cotton: 1 skein of 98, 86, 22, small amount 102
Anchor Lamé: 1 skein gold 300

Beads:
Your own choice

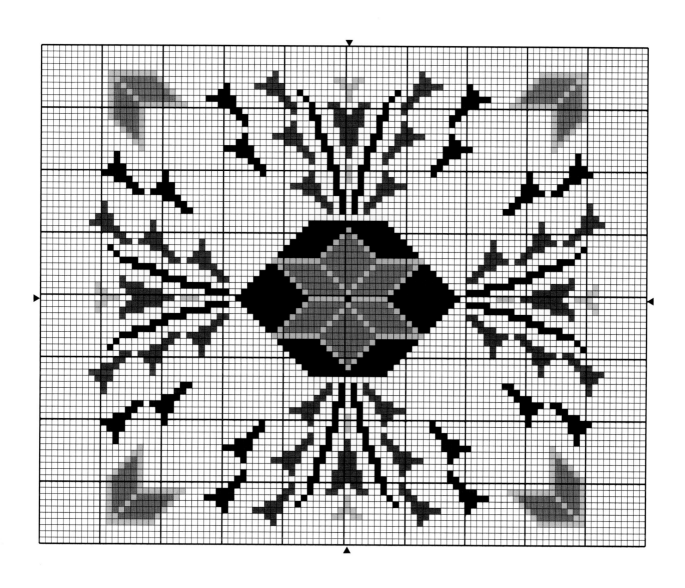

To work the design

Fabric count: 28-count Evenweave worked over 2 threads to give 14-count

Number of strands: 2 of cotton, 3 of Lamé

Stitch count: 85 x 73

Design size: 6¹⁄₁₀ x 5²⁄₁₀in (15.4 x 13.2cm)

Thread required

■	102
■	98
■	86
■	22
■	Lamé 300 Gold†

†Use 3 strands

Designs from Stencils

During special festivals, particularly those connected with Holi or Lord Krishna, priests and their assistants use large paper stencils called 'khaka' and marble dust or coloured powder to create floor decorations, known as 'sanzi', in the inner sanctuaries of the temples. As well as religious symbolism, a wide range of subjects is depicted, including animals, plants, decorative patterns and figures. In the towns and villages, floors, courtyards, gates and doorways are also decorated using a paste of crushed rice and water to make patterns which are then filled with coloured powder.

Decorative floor and wall paintings can be found in many village homes throughout the year, as they are a symbol of welcome and a wish for good luck. They are also used to celebrate marriage, birth, death and the reaching of puberty. Some of the designs, which include patterns, heavenly peacocks, lucky parrots, Tree-of-Life designs and images of the sun, are passed down through families.

I found the shapes of these stencils very attractive, and have developed some of them to create new designs. Each of the individual stencil patterns can be used on its own or repeated to form borders for many projects.

Animal Bell-Pull

Animals play a large part in Indian culture. Four animals looking towards the four corners of the world feature repeatedly throughout Indian art. A lion represents Buddha and looks towards the north, a bull looks west, an elephant to the east and a horse to the south.

This bell-pull does not feature all of these animals but is formed of a collection of animal and border stencils. As the shapes are important and need to be distinct, I chose not to use a variety of colours. However, they would look equally fine stitched in variegated thread or in alternative colours.

Working the design

Overcast the edges to prevent fraying, then work the design in the centre of the fabric using two strands of cotton and three strands of lamé worked over two threads.

Materials required

Fabric: 28-count pale grey Jobelan
11 x 40in (28 x 102cm)
Threads:
Anchor Stranded Cotton: 4 skeins 401,
1 skein 13,
Anchor Lamé: 1 skein 303, 318
Beads:
Mill Hill: Antique Glass 03043

Cross-Stitch Designs from India

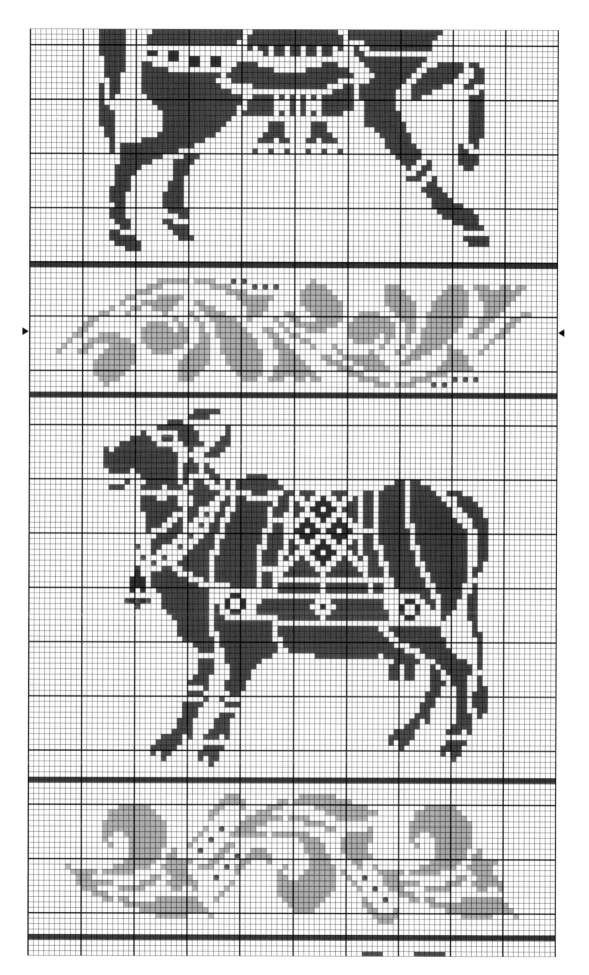

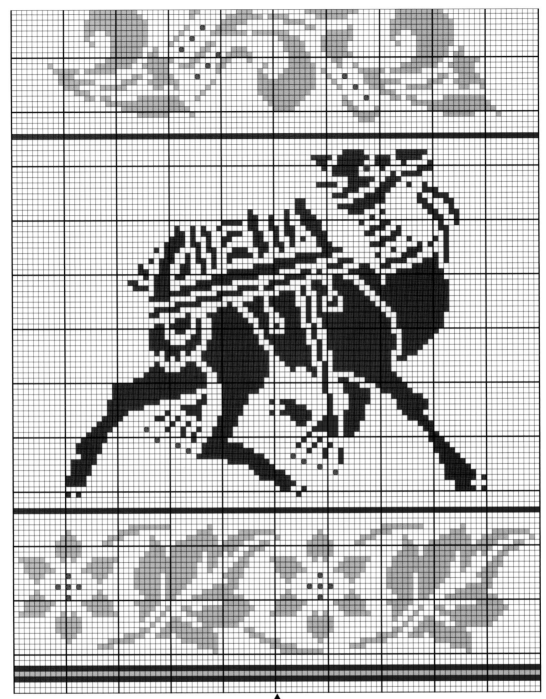

See note on page 2

See note on page 2

To work the design

Fabric count: 28-count worked over 2 threads to give 14-count

Number of strands: 2 of stranded cotton, 3 of lamé

Stitch count: 100 x 424

Design size: 7¹⁄₁₀ x 30³⁄₁₀in (18.1 x 76.9cm)

Thread required

▨	401
▨	Lamé 318 Red
▨	13
▨	Lamé 303 Gold†
▨	Mill Hill beads Antique Glass 03043
—	401*

*Backstitch †Use 3 strands

Peacock Stencil Picture

This is a simple design with minimal use of colour. A touch of silver thread, in addition to some bugle and round beads, adds an element of flamboyancy, though, that is in keeping with the nature of the peacock.

Working the design

Overcast the edges to prevent fraying, then work the design in the centre of the fabric using two strands of cotton and three strands of lamé worked over two threads. Fasten four pearl, white or silver beads onto the head feathers. Then, using one strand of navy thread, stitch the bugle beads to represent the feather shafts. I found it helpful to lightly draw an arc in tailor's chalk to assist with the positioning of the beads. I alternated blue and green bugles on the inner circle and used white on the outer circle.

Thread required

▇	189
▇	1349
▨	Lamé 301 Silver
▇	187
▇	185
	Pearl, silver or white bead

Materials required

Fabric: 28-count Jobelan or Brittney
14 x 14in (35.5 x 35.5cm)

Threads:
Anchor Stranded Cotton: 1 skein of 185, 187, 189, 1349
Anchor Lamé: small amount silver 301

Beads:
Small white, pearl or silver x 4
Bugle beads: white x 26, blue x 10, green x 9

To work the design

Fabric count: 28-count navy blue Jobelan or Brittney worked over 2 threads to give 14-count

Number of strands: 2 of cotton, 3 of Lamé

Stitch count: 136 x 147

Design size: 9⁷⁄₁₀ x 10⁵⁄₁₀in (24.7 x 26.7cm)

Cross-Stitch Designs from India

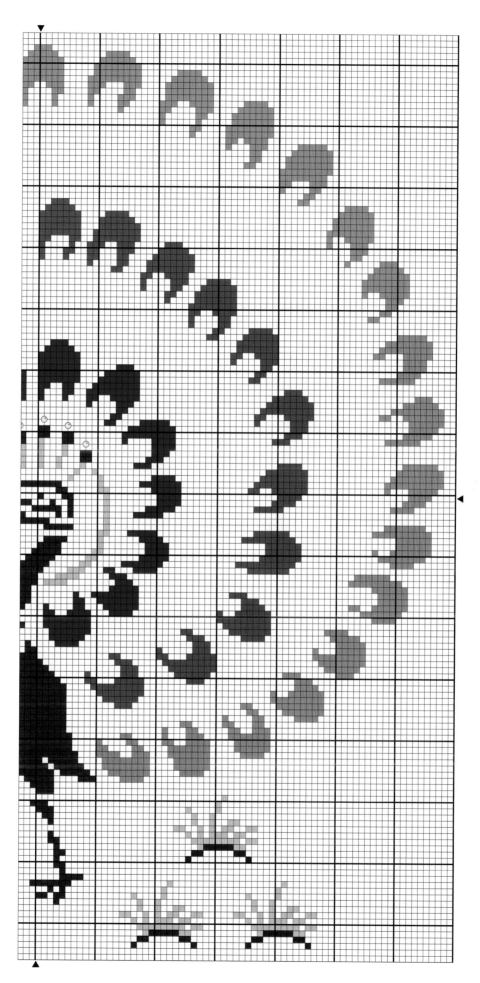

Stencil Lady Picture

For this picture I took inspiration from a stencil of a lady, a background based on an Andhra Pradesh pen-work ('kalam') textile print, and a border from a painting. The lady is depicted using a spray of coloured powder during a festival.

The background design is worked using a single strand of gold lamé which, when complete, really manages to set off the rest of the picture.

I have designed a matching picture of a man with a drum, also at the festival, and included the chart so that you are able to stitch the two as a pair if you wish.

Working the design

Overcast the edges to prevent fraying, then work the design in the centre of the fabric using two strands of cotton and three strands of lamé for the border, and one strand of lamé for the background over two threads.

Materials required

Fabric: 28-count Jobelan 13 x 18in (33 x 46cm)

Threads:
Anchor Stranded Cotton: 2 skeins 403, 46
Anchor Lamé: 1 skein gold 303

To work the design

Fabric count: 28-count Jobelan or Brittney worked over 2 threads to give 14-count

Number of strands: 2 of cotton, either 1 or 3 of lamé as shown on the chart

Stitch count: 125 x 194

Design size: 8⁹⁄₁₀ x 13⁹⁄₁₀in (22.7 x 35.2cm)

Thread required

■	403
	Lamé 303 Gold
	Lamé 303 Gold†
■	46

Cross-Stitch Designs from India

Peacock Stencil Gift–Tag

When I saw this small stencil I envisaged it stitched as a miniature, so I chose to stitch it on 22-count fabric using only one strand of Coats Reflecta, which is a densely coloured shiny thread. It just fits into an aperture with a maximum size of 1½in (4cm), so with the addition of a bow and ribbon it makes a lovely gift-tag.

Working the design

Overcast the edges to prevent fraying, then work the design in the centre of the fabric using a single thread.

Thread required

■■■	Coats Reflecta 316
——	Coats Reflecta 316*

*Backstitch

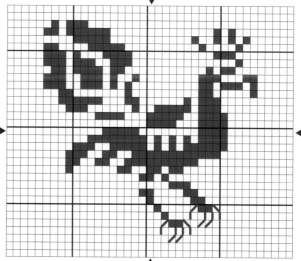

Materials required

Fabric: 22-count evenweave fabric 3in (8cm) square

Threads:
Coats Reflecta: 316

To work the design

Fabric count: 22-count worked over every thread

Number of strands: 1

Stitch count: 29 x 29

Design size: 1³⁄₁₀ x 1³⁄₁₀in (3.3 x 3.3cm)

Paisley Designs

In East Bengal (now known as Bangladesh) Mughal women with very little money spent much of their time making embroidered and patchwork bedspreads and furnishings from discarded saris. They used the fabric as a base for dense embroidery, which acted as a reinforcement for the thin, worn-out material and made it last longer. They also (and this seems almost unbelievable today) unpicked threads from the saris to use for the embroidery! It is frustrating enough having to unpick some stitches that are wrong, never mind having to unpick all your threads!

These 'kantha' artists, as they were known, developed a pattern style that consisted of a lotus medallion surrounded by a border of flowers. In the corners they put 'Kalka' motifs. They are considered to be the origin of the paisley designs now associated with Scotland, and were introduced to the Western world in the eighteenth century.

Many Indian designs have paisleys within them. I have adapted some of these to form the designs in this chapter.

Green Paisley Picture

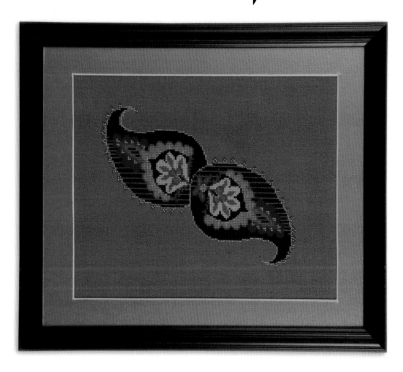

The inspiration for this design came from an Andhra Pradesh sketch that was to be used for textile printing. My original intention was for it to be made up into a book cover, but when I had completed it I decided it was too striking to be on a bookshelf out of sight, so I made it into a picture instead. The colour scheme of green, gold, orange and brown is typically Indian. The gold beads add a finishing touch.

Working the design

Overcast the edges to prevent fraying, then work the design in the centre of the fabric using two strands over two threads. When the stitching is complete, stitch on the beads using a single thread.

Materials required

Fabric: 28-count green Jobelan or Brittney 16 x 18in (41 x 46cm)

Threads:
Anchor Stranded Cotton: 2 skeins 45
1 skein 305, 307, 308, 330, 335, 341
Anchor Lamé: small amount gold 303

Beads:
Mill Hill: Glass Seed 02011

To work the design

Fabric count: 28-count green Jobelan or Brittney worked over 2 threads to give 14-count

Number of strands: 2 of stranded cotton, 3 of Lamé

Stitch count: 94 x 121

Design size: 5%10 x 7%10in (14.9 x 19.2cm)

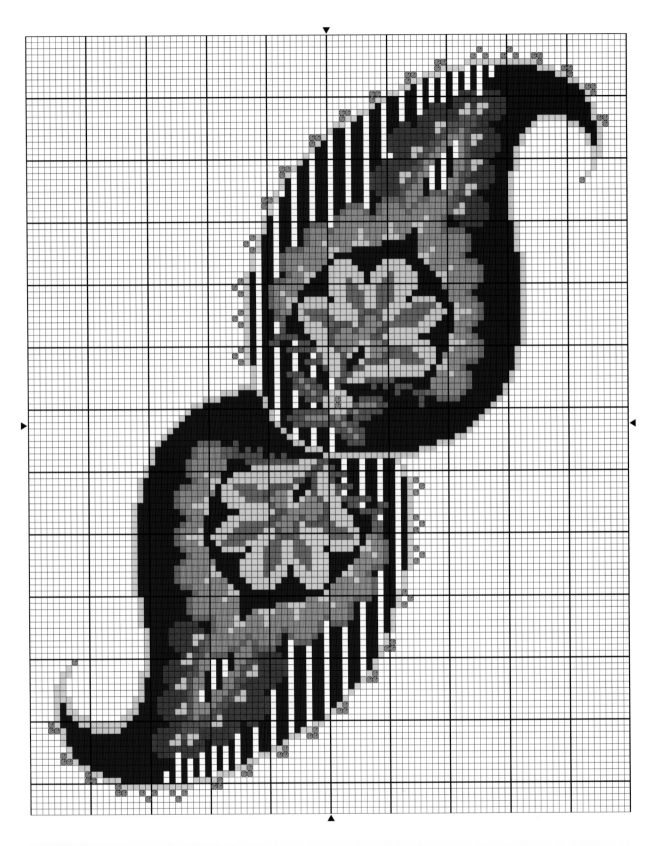

Thread required

■	45		▨	330
▨	305		■	341
▨	335		▨	Lamé 303 Gold†
▨	308		▨	Mill Hill beads Glass Seed 02011
▨	307			†Use 3 strands

Pink and Purple Paisley Picture

From the hundreds of paisley designs to be found, I picked out four from various regions in India that I thought would link together and adapted them to form this picture, although the design would look equally good made up as a bell-pull.

I used a 19-count fabric, but it could also be stitched on a larger count, as it contains a lot of detail. Another variation would be to stitch one, or all, of the designs to make individual pictures, cushion centres or cards.

I used a variegated pink and a variegated blue thread, obtainable from De Haviland.

Materials required

Fabric: 19-count Easistitch 10 x 21in (25.5 x 53cm) – this allows for extra at the sides for framing.

Threads:
Anchor Stranded Cotton: 1 skein 85, 87, 98, 100, 101, 108, 110, 117, 118, 941
Variegated pink: see text
Variegated blue: see text

Motifs:
Optional

To work the design

Fabric count: 19-count Easistitch worked over every thread

Number of strands: 2

Stitch count: 71 x 270

Design size: 3⁷/₁₀ x 14²/₁₀in (9.5 x 36.1cm)

See note on page 2

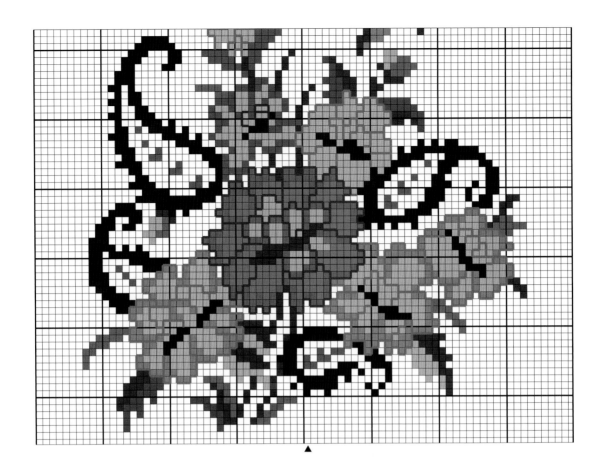

threads, but one strand 110 and one strand 87 of Anchor stranded cotton used together would be a substitute for the pink, and 110 and 118 for the blue.

As a finishing touch, I stitched on small gold paisley motifs, cut from a length of motifs that I found in a haberdashery store. I have seen these lengths in several places, including needlework shows, so you may be able to find them. If not, the picture would still look good without them, or you could substitute gold beads stitched in a paisley shape.

Working the design

Overcast the edges to prevent fraying, then work the design in the centre of the fabric using two strands over every thread. Add the motifs of your choice.

Thread required

	117
	118
	Multi-blue
	98
	100
	101
	Multi-pink
	87
	110
	941
	108
	85
	100*
	941*
	101*

*Backstitch

Note

If you use Easistitch, it frays very easily. It is therefore inadvisable to start stitching before the edges are secured.

Paisley Card

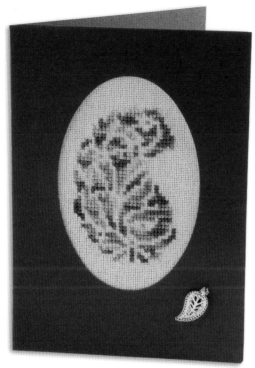

This design was based on a stencil for textile printing from Rajasthan. Stitched on 14-count, it will fit cards with an aperture not less than 2¾ x 4in (7 x 10.5cm).

Working the design

Stitch the design in the centre of the fabric using two strands over two threads. Glue on a small paisley motif.

Thread required

▓▓▓	1355

◆ Materials required

Fabric: 28-count Jobelan or Brittney 4 x 6in (10.5 x 15cm)

Threads:
Anchor Stranded Cotton: 1 skein of 1355
Mountain Stream
Optional motif
Card with aperture not less than 2¾ x 4in (7 x 10.5cm)

◆ To work the design

Fabric count: 28-count Jobelan or Brittney worked over 2 threads to give 14-count

Number of strands: 2

Stitch count: 29 x 43

Design size: 2¹⁄₁₀ x 3¹⁄₁₀in (5.3 x 7.8cm)

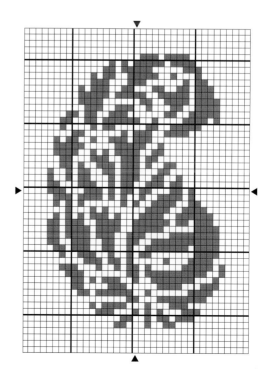

Paisley Table Centre

This design is adapted from an old stencil. By using a variegated thread the pattern is emphasized.

Although I have stitched it on fine-count fabric for use as a centrepiece for a display table, if it were worked on 14-count, the design would measure approximately 10in (25.5cm), enough for a small cushion without a border.

Working the design

Overcast the edges to prevent fraying, then work the design in the centre of the fabric using a single strand over every thread. When complete, fasten Vilene on the back and cut out a circle with a 3½in (9cm) diameter, then stitch lace around the edge.

Materials required
Fabric: 22-count 10 x 10in (25.5 x 25.5cm)
Threads:
Anchor Stranded Cotton: 2 skeins of variegated thread or 1 skein of De Haviland variegated thread

To work the design
Fabric count: 22-count fabric worked over every thread
Number of strands: 1
Stitch count: 143 x 143
Design size: $6\frac{5}{10}$ x $6\frac{5}{10}$in (16.5 x 16.5cm)

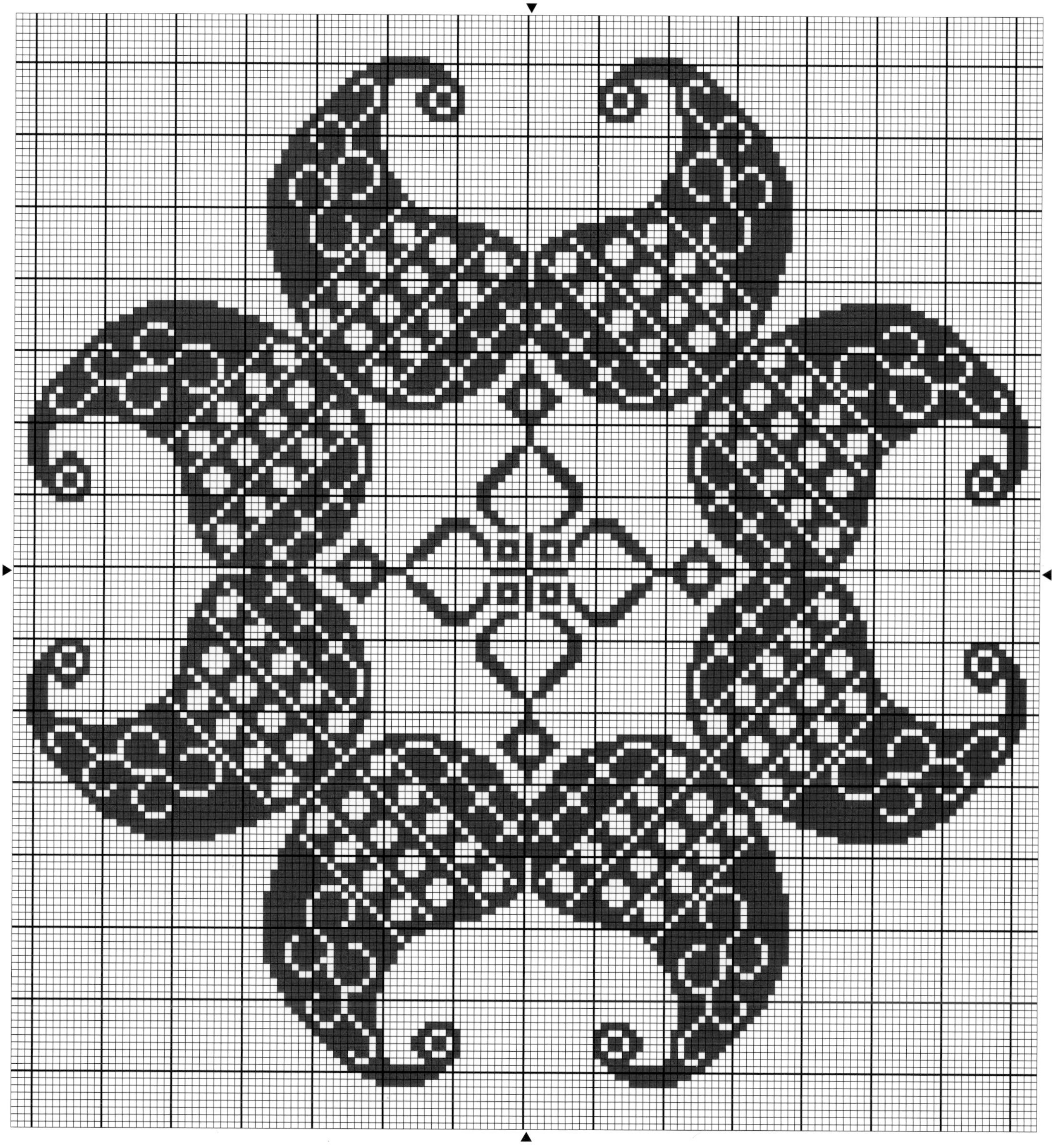

Thread required

Variegated thread of choice

Elephant Designs

The Mughals were interested in elephants and revered them. They were seen as the epitome of strength and, as such, in Indian temple architecture elephants were often depicted supporting the structures. Not only were they useful for transporting heavy loads through jungles, over mountains and across rivers, they were found to be intelligent, faithful creatures and invaluable in battle.

An elephant was often kept inside the temples to head religious processions and carry the temple deities. Misfortune came from harming the elephant in any way, while blessings were bestowed on anyone feeding it.

The Emperor Akbar reportedly had over 100 elephants for use in battle, ceremonial transportation and for the sport of elephant fighting. This was an exciting event for the spectator, but often led to the death of the elephant and its rider. The life of the rider was put so much at risk that his wife would remove and destroy any marital ornaments and jewellery and act as a widow even before the fighting had begun.

Elephants also feature strongly in Indian mythology. One story tells how, while the gods and demons were searching the oceans for the elixir of life to make them immortal, nine jewels came to the surface, one of which was an elephant. Thereafter, the elephant was considered to be as precious as a jewel and treated as such.

Another such story tells of how the elephant was the chosen carriage for all of the gods, and one special elephant, great in size and with ten tusks, transported Indra, the king of the gods.

It is also believed that the birth of the Prophet of Peace, Buddha, occurred after Buddha's mother dreamt of a white elephant. Buddhists believed that white or light-coloured elephants, which are rare, were the most precious of all and were treated as holy and automatically became the property of the ruler.

As a result of their importance, images of elephants can be found in Indian paintings, metalwork, textile designs and ceramics, many of which inspired the designs in this chapter.

Elephant Pictures

These designs have been made up into pictures but they would work just as well as wall-hangings. The elephant depicted in the first project was adapted from a Bijapur watercolour painting from the mid-seventeenth century, which showed Muhammed Adil Shah and Ikhlas Khan riding highly decorated elephants. The elephant in the second picture is from a wall-hanging from Gujarat. As I only saw a black and white image of it, I could let my imagination run riot on the use of colours.

The heraldic-looking base patterns are from 'torans'. Torans are friezes that hang above the principal doorways in a house, especially during special festivals. They have variously shaped embroidered pennants hanging down, which represent mango leaves, symbolizing good luck and welcome. Each picture is composed of an elephant

To work the design

Fabric count: 28-count Evenweave worked over 2 threads

Number of strands: 2

Stitch count: 105 x 137

Design size: 7⁵⁄₁₀ x 9⁸⁄₁₀in (19 x 24.9cm)

Materials required

Fabric: 28-count Evenweave 19 x 14in (48.5 x 35.5cm)

Threads:
Anchor Stranded Cotton: 1 skein of 235, 400, 236, 134, 298, 46, small amounts of 403, 386
Anchor Lamé: 1 skein red 318, gold 303

Beads:
Mill Hill: Glass Seed 02011 x 129

and two borders, and any of these could be used separately. The bright, colourful designs incorporate ribbon, sequins, beads, tassels and shisha mirrors, and are fun to stitch. The red and gold ribbon I have used is ideal, as it features elephants. However, any gold or red ribbon would look attractive. The red sequin band is readily available but you could thread loops of beads as an alternative.

Working the design

Overcast the edges to prevent fraying. When stitching the design, you must remember to leave enough room above the elephants for the ribbon. I measured 10in (25.5cm) down from the top of the fabric

and 7in (18cm) in from the side and used this as the centre of the stitching. I stitched the ribbon with the bottom edge 1½in (4cm) above the elephant's head with the sequin band below.

I made small tassels using eleven wraps of lamé over a 2½in (6cm) card, then trimmed each to 1½in (4cm). If you are making a wall-hanging and do not have the restriction of the frame glass to consider, you could make chunkier, longer tassels with beads threaded on the ends, and replace the flower sequins with small gold bells. You could perhaps also fasten a red and gold cord down the sides.

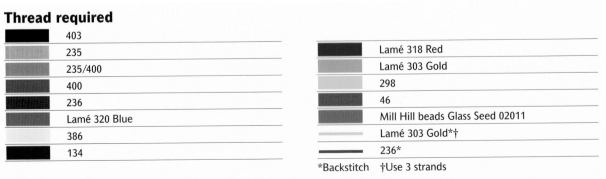

Thread required

■	403
▨	235
▨	235/400
▨	400
▨	236
▨	Lamé 320 Blue
▨	386
■	134

▨	Lamé 318 Red
▨	Lamé 303 Gold
▨	298
▨	46
▨	Mill Hill beads Glass Seed 02011
—	Lamé 303 Gold*†
—	236*

*Backstitch   †Use 3 strands

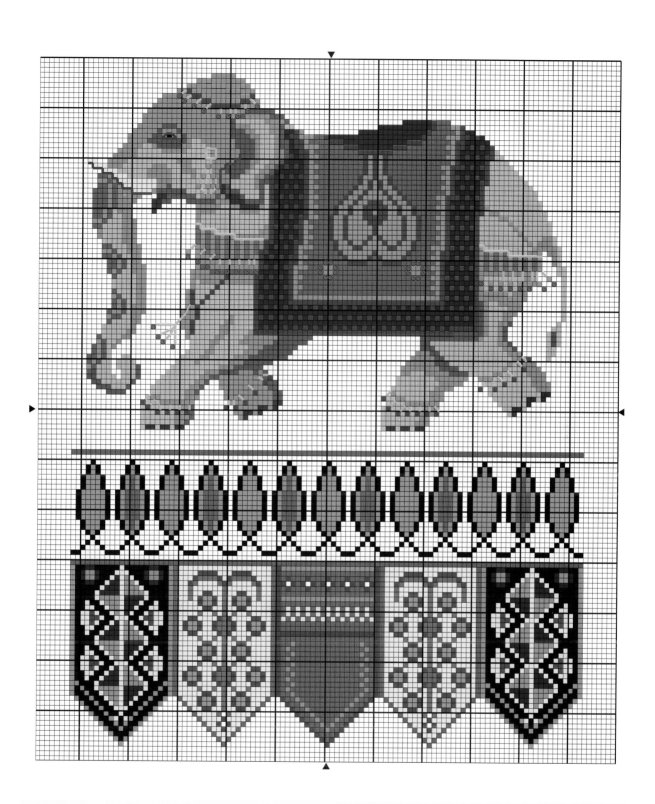

Thread required

■	403
	235
	235/400
	400
	236
	Lamé 320 Blue
	386
	112

	134
	Lamé 318 Red
	Lamé 303 Gold
	Lamé 322 Green†
	230
	Mill Hill beads Glass Seed 02011
	Lamé 303 Gold*†
—	236*

*Backstitch   †Use 3 strands

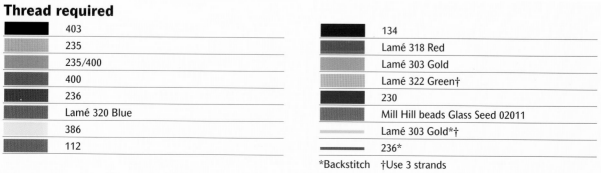

Elephant Bookmark

This fun bookmark is made up of a simple repetitive stencil design, but you could also stitch a single elephant as a motif or repetitively to form a horizontal band of running elephants. Only small amounts of thread are required, and they can be in any colour, so it is a good project for using up remnants of thread. I used a ready-made bookmark from Framecraft Miniatures, then added matching beads at the bottom.

Working the design

Stitch the design in the centre of the bookmark using two strands over every thread.

Materials required

Fabric: Ready-made 18-count bookmark from Framecraft Miniatures

Threads:
Anchor Stranded Cotton: 1 skein of 178, 45

To work the design

Fabric count: 18-count over every thread

Number of strands: 2

Stitch count: 29 x 110

Design size: 1⁹⁄₁₀ x 6¹⁄₁₀in (4.1 x 15.5cm)

Thread required

■	178
■	45

Elephant Designs

Instructions for Making Up Projects

When you have finished stitching, check you haven't missed any stitches or blocks of stitching, as this is easily done. You can check tapestry by holding the stitching up to the light. Missing stitches become obvious.

Evenweave fabrics can be ironed on the wrong side with a medium iron using a damp cloth to prevent scorching. Padding the board with a towel or ironing pad will give the best result because it makes the stitching stand out from the base fabric. Work done on Aida or Jobelan with Anchor stranded cotton can be washed using a mild detergent and hot water (as hot as the hand will stand as the hot water sets fast the colours) then rinsed thoroughly. Occasionally there may be a slight bleeding from darker colours – just keep rinsing until the water runs clear. The embroidery should be ironed while still slightly damp following the above directions.

Wool, silk or canvas embroideries must not be washed but they can be dry-cleaned. They may need to be stretched back into shape when the stitching is complete. They can then be sprayed with fabric protector.

Pictures

Complete the embroidery ready for making-up. Lace the picture onto thick card or 3mm (⅛in) MDF using quilting thread, which is less likely to break when you pull it tight. Start lacing across the back from the centre out each time, then tighten the lacing and finish off the thread. Always make sure that if the stitching is on a light colour you either line the board with white paper or paint it white before fastening on the picture. Professional framers frequently offer a stretching service, too.

Bell-Pulls and Wall-Hangings

Prepare the embroidery ready for making-up. Decide the length and width that you need your hanging to be. If you have special ends, you will not have much choice as these dictate the size, but if you are using a cane or dowelling they can be any size.

Trim any excess fabric, leaving 4in (10cm) at the top and bottom and 1in (2.5cm) at each side. If I have used an evenweave fabric, I always iron a piece of Vilene on the back before turning the edges, to give the hanging more weight. Turn the long sides to the back and slip-stitch in place, then turn over a hem at the top and bottom, making sure that you leave a slot for the rods to go through. You may wish to neaten the back by slip-stitching a silk or cotton backing onto it. Then slot the rods through.

An alternative to slip-stitching the edges if you have used an evenweave fabric is to secure the long sides with strips of 1in (2.5cm) Vilene ironed onto the back, catching in the side turnings.

Adding a heavy tassel or beads gives weight to the bottom, which can help it to hang better.

Cards

When the stitching is complete and ready to be made up, first iron a piece of Vilene, slightly larger than the aperture, onto the back of the design, then you can cut it without the fabric fraying. Allowing a good margin all round, cut the fabric to fit centrally in the aperture. Glue the stitching into position, using a glue stick or double-sided tape, unless the card is already glued. Then glue the outer edges of the left-hand third of the card and press down firmly to secure the embroidery and cover the back.

Cushions

The instructions below are for all types of cushion, including pin and pot-pourri, as they are all made up in the same way.

Pincushions, pot-pourri cushions and decorative cushions that will not need frequent washing:

Decide on the size that you wish your completed cushion to be, then, centreing the stitching, trim the excess canvas or evenweave, leaving at least 1½in (4cm) on all sides. Cut a piece of backing fabric the same size, and, with right sides facing, tack and stitch the two pieces together, leaving a sufficient opening on the bottom edge for the cushion to be turned through to the right side. Trim the excess seam allowance and snip across the corners to remove any

bulk, then turn the cushion right side out. Insert the cushion pad, or stuff the cushion, then slip-stitch the gap closed.

Cushions with Removable Covers

Work from * to * above.

Cut a piece of backing fabric that is the same width, but 8in (20cm) longer than the required size. Cut this in half widthways and turn a narrow double hem along one width of each piece. With right sides facing up and hems towards each other, overlap these halves to make the backing the same size as the cushion front. Tack together. With right sides facing, tack and stitch the front and back together without leaving a gap. Trim the excess fabric, clip across the corners, then turn through to the right side using the central overlap. Insert the cushion pad.

Bookmarks

I always back the stitching on bookmarks with iron-on Vilene before finishing it off to give it more body, but this is optional.

If working on a ready-made bookmark, first check that the pattern you wish to stitch will fit onto the bookmark, then stitch the design.

If working on Aida band, stitch the design and then turn a small hem at the top and the bottom of the band. Band fabric comes in a variety of sizes, so do make sure you choose one that is appropriate for the size of pattern you intend to stitch.

If you are making the bookmark from fabric, first edge the fabric to prevent fraying, then stitch the design. Slipstitch a small hem at the top, bottom and sides.

To finish, stitch either ribbon or fabric on the back to make it neater, then add a tassel if you wish. Remember not to add any embellishments that might damage the pages.

Thread Conversion Chart

This conversion chart is for guidance only, as exact comparisons are not always possible.

Anchor	DMC	Madeira	Anchor	DMC	Madeira	Anchor	DMC	Madeira
1	blanc	2401	152	939	1009	339	920	312
9	352	303	168	518/597	1108	340	919	313
10	351	406	175	794	907	341	355	314
11	350	213	177	792	905	361	738	2013
13	347	211	178	791	904	368	436	2011
20	3777	2502	185	964	1112	369	435	2010
22	815	2501	186	959	1113	376	842	1910
40	899	2707	187	958	1114	386	746	2512
41	335	611	188	943	2706	398	415	1802
45	814	2606	189	991	2705	400	317	1714
46	6566	210	205	912	1213	403	310	2400
47	304	510	230	910	1303	410	995	1102
55	604	614	235	414	1801	843	3012	1606
68	3687	604	236	3799	1713	846	936	1507
69	3685	2609	245	701	1305	876	503	1703
70	*	2608	246	986	1404	878	501	1205
74	3354	606	266	470	1502	894	3326	813
75	3733	505	267	469	1503	899	3022	1906
76	961	505	268	937	1504	914	407	2310
85	3609	710	269	895	1507	969	816	809
86	3608	709	276	3770	2314	970	3726	2609
87	3607	708	278	472	1414	972	915	2609
98	553	712	279	734	1610	1001	976	2302
100	327	2714	280	581	1611	1012	948	305
101	550	713	281	731	1612	1013	3778	2310
102	*	2709	298	972	107	1014	355	2502
108	210	2711	305	743	109	1019	315	810
109	209	2711	306	725	2514	1027	223	812
110	*	2710	307	783	2514	1028	3685	2608
112	*	2710	308	782	2211	1029	3685	705
117	341	901	316	740	202	1033	932	1710
118	340	902	326	720	309	1034	931	1711
123	3750	914	330	947	205	1035	930	1712
127	823	1008	332	946	207	1036	336	1712
130	809	907	334	606	209	1044	890	1405
131	798	911	335	606	209	1089	996	
150	823	1007	338	921	402	5975	356	401

About the Author

Carol was born in Scarborough, North Yorkshire and, after training as a teacher, lived in the East Riding of Yorkshire for many years with her husband and two daughters. During this time she combined teaching with freelance embroidery designing, working mainly for magazines and kit companies.

She and Alan have recently moved to Leek, Staffordshire, to be nearer their daughters and grandson and to enable them to pursue more easily their hobby of walking in the Staffordshire and Derbyshire Dales.

Carol continues to design and stitch, both for magazines and books.

Index

Cross-Stitch Designs from India

WOODTURNING

Bowl Turning Techniques Masterclass	Tony Boase
Chris Child's Projects for Woodturners	Chris Child
Decorating Turned Wood: The Maker's Eye	Liz & Michael O'Donnell
Green Woodwork	Mike Abbott
Keith Rowley's Woodturning Projects	Keith Rowley
Making Screw Threads in Wood	Fred Holder
Segmented Turning: A Complete Guide	Ron Hampton
Turned Boxes: 50 Designs	Chris Stott
Turning Green Wood	Michael O'Donnell
Turning Pens and Pencils	Kip Christensen & Rex Burningham
Woodturning: Forms and Materials	John Hunnex
Woodturning: A Foundation Course (New Edition)	Keith Rowley
Woodturning: A Fresh Approach	Robert Chapman
Woodturning: An Individual Approach	Dave Regester
Woodturning: A Source Book of Shapes	John Hunnex
Woodturning Masterclass	Tony Boase

WOODWORKING

Beginning Picture Marquetry	Lawrence Threadgold
Celtic Carved Lovespoons: 30 Patterns	Sharon Littley & Clive Griffin
Celtic Woodcraft	Glenda Bennett
Complete Woodfinishing (Revised Edition)	Ian Hosker
David Charlesworth's Furniture-Making Techniques	David Charlesworth
David Charlesworth's Furniture-Making Techniques – Volume 2	David Charlesworth
Furniture Projects with the Router	Kevin Ley
Furniture Restoration (Practical Crafts)	Kevin Jan Bonner
Furniture Restoration: A Professional at Work	John Lloyd
Green Woodwork	Mike Abbott
Intarsia: 30 Patterns for the Scrollsaw	John Everett
Making Heirloom Boxes	Peter Lloyd
Making Screw Threads in Wood	Fred Holder
Making Woodwork Aids and Devices	Robert Wearing
Mastering the Router	Ron Fox
Pine Furniture Projects for the Home	Dave Mackenzie
Router Magic: Jigs, Fixtures and Tricks to Unleash your Router's Full Potential	Bill Hylton
Router Projects for the Home	GMC Publications
Router Tips & Techniques	Robert Wearing
Routing: A Workshop Handbook	Anthony Bailey
Routing for Beginners	Anthony Bailey
Stickmaking: A Complete Course	Andrew Jones & Clive George
Stickmaking Handbook	Andrew Jones & Clive George
Storage Projects for the Router	GMC Publications
Veneering: A Complete Course	Ian Hosker
Veneering Handbook	Ian Hosker
Woodworking Techniques and Projects	Anthony Bailey
Woodworking with the Router: Professional Router Techniques any Woodworker can Use	Bill Hylton & Fred Matlack

UPHOLSTERY

Upholstery: A Complete Course (Revised Edition)	David James
Upholstery Restoration	David James
Upholstery Techniques & Projects	David James
Upholstery Tips and Hints	David James

DOLLS' HOUSES AND MINIATURES

1/12 Scale Character Figures for the Dolls' House	James Carrington
Americana in 1/12 Scale: 50 Authentic Projects	Joanne Ogreenc & Mary Lou Santovec
The Authentic Georgian Dolls' House	Brian Long
A Beginners' Guide to the Dolls' House Hobby	Jean Nisbett
Celtic, Medieval and Tudor Wall Hangings in 1/12 Scale Needlepoint	Sandra Whitehead
Creating Decorative Fabrics: Projects in 1/12 Scale	Janet Storey
Dolls' House Accessories, Fixtures and Fittings	Andrea Barham
Dolls' House Furniture: Easy-to-Make Projects in 1/12 Scale	Freida Gray
Dolls' House Makeovers	Jean Nisbett
Dolls' House Window Treatments	Eve Harwood
Edwardian-Style Hand-Knitted Fashion for 1/12 Scale Dolls	Yvonne Wakefield
How to Make Your Dolls' House Special: Fresh Ideas for Decorating	Beryl Armstrong
Making 1/12 Scale Wicker Furniture for the Dolls' House	Sheila Smith
Making Miniature Chinese Rugs and Carpets	Carol Phillipson
Making Miniature Food and Market Stalls	Angie Scarr
Making Miniature Gardens	Freida Gray
Making Miniature Oriental Rugs & Carpets	Meik & Ian McNaughton
Making Miniatures: Projects for the 1/12 Scale Dolls' House	Christiane Berridge
Making Period Dolls' House Accessories	Andrea Barham
Making Tudor Dolls' Houses	Derek Rowbottom
Making Upholstered Furniture in 1/12 Scale	Janet Storey
Medieval and Tudor Needlecraft: Knights and Ladies in 1/12 Scale	Sandra Whitehead
Miniature Bobbin Lace	Roz Snowden
Miniature Crochet: Projects in 1/12 Scale	Roz Walters
Miniature Embroidery for the Georgian Dolls' House	Pamela Warner
Miniature Embroidery for the Tudor and Stuart Dolls' House	Pamela Warner
Miniature Embroidery for the 20th-Century Dolls' House	Pamela Warner
Miniature Embroidery for the Victorian Dolls' House	Pamela Warner
Miniature Needlepoint Carpets	Janet Granger
More Miniature Oriental Rugs & Carpets	Meik & Ian McNaughton
Needlepoint 1/12 Scale: Design Collections for the Dolls' House	Felicity Price
New Ideas for Miniature Bobbin Lace	Roz Snowden
Patchwork Quilts for the Dolls' House: 20 Projects in 1/12 Scale	Sarah Williams
Simple Country Furniture Projects in 1/12 Scale	Alison J. White

CRAFTS

Bargello: A Fresh Approach to Florentine Embroidery	Brenda Day
Beginning Picture Marquetry	Lawrence Threadgold
Blackwork: A New Approach	Brenda Day
Celtic Cross Stitch Designs	Carol Phillipson
Celtic Knotwork Designs	Sheila Sturrock
Celtic Knotwork Handbook	Sheila Sturrock
Celtic Spirals and Other Designs	Sheila Sturrock
Celtic Spirals Handbook	Sheila Sturrock
Complete Pyrography	Stephen Poole
Creating Made-to-Measure Knitwear: A Revolutionary Approach to Knitwear Design	Sylvia Wynn
Creative Backstitch	Helen Hall
Creative Log-Cabin Patchwork	Pauline Brown
Creative Machine Knitting	GMC Publications
Cross-Stitch Designs from China	Carol Phillipson
Cross-Stitch Floral Designs	Joanne Sanderson
Decoration on Fabric: A Sourcebook of Ideas	Pauline Brown
Decorative Beaded Purses	Enid Taylor
Designing and Making Cards	Glennis Gilruth
Designs for Pyrography and Other Crafts	Norma Gregory
Dried Flowers: A Complete Guide	Lindy Bird
Exotic Textiles in Needlepoint	Stella Knight
Glass Engraving Pattern Book	John Everett
Glass Painting	Emma Sedman
Handcrafted Rugs	Sandra Hardy
Hobby Ceramics: Techniques and Projects for Beginners	Patricia A. Waller

GARDENING

ART TECHNIQUES

VIDEOS

MAGAZINES

WOODTURNING ♦ WOODCARVING ♦ FURNITURE & CABINETMAKING
THE ROUTER ♦ NEW WOODWORKING ♦ THE DOLLS' HOUSE MAGAZINE
OUTDOOR PHOTOGRAPHY ♦ BLACK & WHITE PHOTOGRAPHY
MACHINE KNITTING NEWS ♦ KNITTING
GUILD OF MASTER CRAFTSMEN NEWS

The above represents a full list of all titles currently published or scheduled to be published.
All are available direct from the Publishers or through bookshops, newsagents and specialist retailers.
To place an order, or to obtain a complete catalogue, contact:

GMC Publications,
Castle Place, 166 High Street, Lewes, East Sussex BN7 1XU United Kingdom
Tel: 01273 488005 Fax: 01273 402866
E-mail: pubs@thegmcgroup.com

Orders by credit card are accepted